EARLY Childhood Development

EARLY Childhood Development

UNIVERSAL PERSPECTIVES BY GLOBAL EXPERTS

EARLY CHILDHOOD DEVELOPMENT FORUM
Compiled by **Dr VASAVVI ACHARJYA**

Vitasta

For all early childhood educators
and parents of the little angels
who dedicate themselves to
giving these children the best in
their early years
And for the little ones who light
up our lives...

Published by
Renu Kaul Verma
Vitasta Publishing Pvt Ltd
2/15, Ansari Road, Daryaganj
New Delhi – 110 002
info@vitastapublishing.com

ISBN 978-81-960413-1-1

First Edition 2023
MRP ₹695

Edited by Mehnaz Hussain
Cover and layout by Somesh Kumar Mishra
Printed by Chaman Enterprises, New Delhi

CONTENTS

PREFACE

The Early Childhood Development Forum (ECDF) founded in 2019 is an initiative of the Debendra Nath Acharya Foundation for Children and Women Welfare (2014) that works towards implementing the best practices for Early Childhood Care and Education. The forum supports children from the marginalised sections of the society, by giving them access to quality education.

Initially the forum was operating in Northeast India but during the pandemic the forum shifted its programs (webinars, educator training, conferences, one-day courses et al.) online thereby, reaching out to a global audience. Early years educators from different parts of the world came under one umbrella and started interacting, brainstorming and sharing the best practices of ECCE with one another, thereby making it possible to create a huge congregation of educators who are aware of suitable and guaranteed approaches to childhood care. A few of these enlightened educators came together to form a close bond and worked dedicatedly towards spreading awareness among parents, early years educators and stakeholders, especially those who touch the lives of children in their early years. Although they are experts settled in different parts of the world, they share one common goal—to better the lives of children in their early years. In fact, Early Childhood Development has been a central point of focus in their lives.

This book is a culmination of many sessions of elaborate discussions and exchange of ideas and experiences from experts dealing with early childhood care. Amrit Nagpal begins her chapter with the historicization of the age-old art of storytelling which is considered to be one of the most potent tools for knowledge delivery for younger children and for creating a connection with the world around them. She discusses the importance of storytelling, the footprints it leaves on the human mind and why it is essential to implant storytelling in our culture and in our learning programs. Storytelling to her has the power to engage and inspire listeners. It is through stories that human minds form and scrutinize their own beliefs as well as distinguish how they correlate with the truths and beliefs of others. Through story listening they gain a better understanding of the world around them and develop new perspectives. The chapter throws light on the art and the science of storytelling for maximum positive outcomes.

Abigail Carr beautifully touches upon how nature provides us with learning spaces sans boundaries and restraints. The environment is our third teacher and learning using nature is a practice since time immemorial. Forest schools are more to be found now and practitioners task themselves with understanding how children of all ages can use nature to learn. Indoor and outdoor experiences are often planned to encourage children to see, touch, smell, and taste the world. But, have we missed something important? Have we knowingly or unknowingly alienated ourselves from nature and almost forgotten about how humans are actually a part of nature? Is there more to how one can view the experiences and the opportunities provided to us by the natural world and their interconnection? Carr explores these questions.

Lidia Tavani provides a study of the outdoor education systems at school—the ways in which the outdoors favour learning processes and promote well-being. It focuses on three specific topics: movement, relationship and inclusive learning processes as an affirmation of one's own person in the relationship with everything that is part of the experience. The keyword is 'reflective exploration' which means learning through processes experienced in the unity and completeness of one's own person.

Kari Sutton's chapter touches upon Emotional Management. It is a common human trait to experience anger, fear, frustration, sadness, rejection, disappointment, jealousy, and guilt at different times. Emotionally healthy people can label their emotions and manage their reactions to external events and strong feelings without yelling, throwing things or damaging property. While they might feel angry, frustrated, sad, anxious, or scared, these feelings don't prevent them from managing the situation well as they have developed emotional agility. Children's ability to understand and manage emotions develops over time. When they are young, children need help with understanding emotions. Her chapter provides key findings from the new field of positive psychology and combines them with valuable knowledge from developmental cognitive neuroscience and emotional intelligence, to provide evidence-based strategies and ideas about how parents and educators can help children develop emotional intelligence and thrive. It provides practical strategies and tools that can immediately be implemented in day-to-day interactions to sow the seeds of emotional well-being in children and help them develop positive habits that will last a lifetime.

Mindfulness is the ability to be fully present in the moment and experience it. The chapter 'Impact of Mindfulness' co-written by me and Girija elaborates on the benefits of mindfulness practices for both children and adults. Mindfulness practices should be introduced to children from the early years and this may be done in various ways. In this world full of chaos children need to learn emotion management, resilience, stress management, etc.

Julie Robinson and Mandy Worsley's combined experience, passion and drive have led to the development and creation of a chapter in this book, which focuses on skills that encourage learning how to use positive self-talk and how we can begin to use this to make a difference in our children's health and well-being. It would help readers learn how to develop the best mindset for their children to help them to reach their true potential.

Simran Ballani's chapter 'Etiquette Learning and Public Speaking' in the early years have been a passion project for the author for over a decade now. ELPS curriculum has been designed in such a manner that it instils responsibility and confidence at a crucial stage of development in a child's life. Her chapter gives us a glimpse of how the implementation of this curriculum has transformed the lives of these little ones and their families. Early years have always been a subject of study and research but the author fell in love with the richness and depth of implementing basic life skills as a part of their everyday learning.

Early childhood educators across the world have many things in common. Some of the most important bonds include supporting children to self-regulate in positive ways, communicate effectively and engage with learning by providing rich, open-ended opportunities to explore, imagine, take risks and flourish. Dr Sue Allingham and Dr Kathryn Murray in their study provides insight into what children need in order to develop holistic well-being and how they communicate through their behaviours. They explore how children learn to regulate emotions and build independence and identity. They look at practical ways to facilitate and support the communication of the child's needs using the Leuven Scales to assess emotions and by implementing a Brain-SET environment that aligns the developing brain to the learning spaces.

Another chapter on conscious parenting written by Charlotte Hannah explores the role of the inner child of the adult whilst engaging in a parent-child relationship. The chapter invites the reader to question their own childhoods and self-limiting beliefs, in order to bring more conscious awareness to raising a child. It encourages the provision of a conscious environment in the home.

'Parents as Partners in Early Childhood Education' written by Azura Abrasid, throws light on parenting as a shared responsibility. Positive parent partnership has been shown in studies that it improves children's academic achievement, social competencies, and emotional well-being.

This chapter is about the intensive work between Early Childhood Education practitioners and parents. It explores why it is important, how the relationship can be improved, and what are the challenges in this partnership. The chapter would be of interest to any practitioner who works with parents and wants to extend their practice in this area, as well as parents who require valuable resource in understanding the parental partnership in improving their child's learning and development.

Dr Vasavvi Acharjya
Founder Chairperson of
Early Childhood Development Forum

ACKNOWLEDGEMENTS

This book arose from the competent and extensive research of Early Childhood educators from across the globe. I am grateful to all the researchers and practitioners who came together and committed their time and employed their skills to add to the existing knowledge on Early Childhood development, and hence, contributed in bringing smiles on the faces of the young ones.

I am very grateful to Mehnaz Hussain, whose editing skills unfolded the book in a way that fulfilled its intent and scope. She did an incredible job and extended warmth in bringing the book to its final form. I want to extend my acknowledgements to Ridhima Gandhi, who provided steadfast support in the production of the book. I also want to thank Renu Kaul Verma of Vitasta Publishing, who has been crucial to the publishing of the book, whose encouragement and guidance resulted in this book. My special word of gratitude to designer Somesh Kumar Mishra for the vibrant and beautiful cover design and wonderful layout. Lastly, a big thank you to all Early Years educators who are dedicated in working for our beautiful children and imparting them quality learning experiences and members, friends, and well-wishers of the Early Childhood Development Forum.

Amrit Nagpal
Educational Consultant, Former National Head of Preschools & ECCEd. at Birla Open Minds Education Pvt Ltd

Amrit Nagpal is an enthusiastic and energetic Early Years professional with a Master's in Education from James Cook University. She has a Diploma in Enrichment Studies (Phonics, Music and Movement, and Speech and Drama) from The College of Teachers, UK and a Diploma in TESOL from Global TESOL College, Canada. She has over 15 years of experience in Pre-Primary and Primary teaching, remedial teaching, content designing, curriculum planning, and training pre-service and in-service teachers.

ONE

THE SCIENCE BEHIND THE ART OF STORYTELLING

OUR GRANDPARENTS told exciting stories that piqued the interest of young minds. They shared moments and experiences collected in their memory, which eventually bridged generational gaps and created stronger bonds amongst the members of a family. Progressive educators applied a similar 'story telling' model for pedagogy, in order to educate about challenging concepts in various domains. These stories ignited a light, forming lasting memories which can be applied to solve everyday problems, ensure survival, and pass on their wisdom to other generations.

Some stories have survived for hundreds of years and are still in circulation. Initially they were a part of the oral tradition, meaning they have been in circulation as a result of telling and retelling. Later, however, story tellers began to write down their stories. Not that we wouldn't want to hear stories told out loud; we still love them!

Stories are powerful and are an integral part of every culture. They teach values, tell us about our histories, entertain us, make us laugh or cry, and many more. Telling stories is a huge part of what connects us to one another. Stories are not just fictional narratives but can be used for educational purposes, such as to illustrate science and math. According to Bruner (1986), narrative strives to put timeless miracles into the particulars of experience and to locate the experience in time and place. Stories engage our thinking, emotional and imagination part of the brain all at once. As listeners we participate in a story with both our minds and bodies, as we enter the narrative world and react to it. They are woven into the fabric of our lives in ways we may not be aware of. Stories help teachers reach novices in ways they cannot with other strategies. They bring incongruent information to life in a meaningful way. You probably have your own favourite stories—they could be stories about your family that you have heard from your grandparents or perhaps, are books you have read over and over.

When someone tells a story, the listener's brain waves always synchronize with the storyteller. Listening to a narrative also duly activates regions of the brain. According to former research, this activation involves deciphering or imagining a person's intentions and perspective (Paul J. Zak, Ph.D. 2015). Listening to stories activates neural activity in the human brain by increasing it five-folds.

According to an analysis from a research study, patients in coma at times like the acquainted voices of dear ones, which can facilitate the awakening of the unconscious brain and pace up the recovery process. The results of a cooperative study disclosed that the impact of acknowledged voices telling a patient acquainted stories hold on in memory. Listening to the stories, trigger the release of neurochemical oxytocin. Oxytocin is also called the love drug. Until a few years ago, we were only aware that oxytocin is released when a mother is with her child. However, research findings confirm that listening to stories also triggers the release of oxytocin, thereby, allowing the listeners to acknowledge and experience their emotions, all the while reclaiming and recollecting memory.

For instance, Kumar Sanu, the Indian singer claims that the song *Jab koi baat bigad jaaye* from the film *Jurm* (1990) is rather miraculous.

'The song has helped cure cancer patients in the city. The doctor's decision is it is a miracle. Patients keep noting it on loop. It appears to possess Shakti (power) and awakens the body's healing powers.'

He also adds that this particular song has been helpful to a bank manager's wife in Mumbai who was diagnosed with Breast Cancer.

'The song incorporates a positive vibe. It tells you to measure not meant to be frittered. It provides you courage–a boost, which works as medication.'

How storytelling has progressed?

So long there have been people on this planet, there have been stories. We are surrounded by stories every day—films and pictures tell stories; songs too tell stories. Teachers in school provide lessons which are often stories. When you have a conversation about what happened to you a while ago with your friend, you are telling a story. Can you think of the last story you heard? It can be something you heard a few minutes ago!

The history of storytelling dates back to the age when cave dwellers used pigment to paint on walls with their hands to create stories, i.e., to thousands of years. The Chauvet-Pont-d'Arc Cave in the mountains of Southern France contains cave drawings which date back to 30,000 years ago. On the walls of the cave, explorers found paintings depicting the prehistoric period. The cave drawings tell us stories about early men encountering mammoths, rhinos and lions and their everyday activities of using homemade weapons. This was how early men used to communicate, forming an unspoken and unwritten language.

Moving forward, ancient Greeks carved their language into walls to tell how history has evolved. They lived on islands and fished for food. They discovered several ways to use their tools to carve messages into slates and tombs. Their stories were documented in oral literatures for thousands of years. The Greeks are also the first known civilization to develop extensively the act of writing and to apply it to storytelling in order to compose poems and exchange messages. They used birds such as pigeons to deliver these pressing messages in times of war and celebration.

There was then a shift to words formed into narratives, such as written, typed and printed stories. The narrative voice in writing speaks volumes about each culture. Over the subsequent several centuries, the art of writing and storytelling would evolve and develop into cohesive works such as the Bible and the works of William Shakespeare. Though the

Bible was written back in 1300 BC with stories, myths and legends about gods, prophets and kings. They were tales and lessons with a religious purpose that people learnt through oral storytelling before these stories were penned down. William Shakespeare, the incredible writer, actor, and poet born in 1564 wrote 37 plays during his lifetime including the famous *Romeo and Juliet.* Shakespeare was a huge stepping stone in building stories and the art of narrating them because his work was so expansive and was relatable to everyone. To this day, Shakespeare is still the most performed playwright of all time and his works are continuously adapted for films.

Telling a story is a tangible instance of how legends and myths make storytelling much more valuable to an audience. They eventually came to be known as fairy tales. This started in France. Many fairy tales which were passed from one generation to the next through oral storytelling began to be preserved on paper. The tales were mostly written with keeping children in mind and were created to teach children basic life lessons. One such popular story is of *Hansel and Gretel* which was meant to scare children from wandering off in the forest.

As generations pass by, the tradition of storytelling gets stronger and tales and myths are created with new innovations, often with the use of modern technology. In 1690, first newspaper was published which shook the world. Later, in 1826, the first printed photograph was taken by Joshep Niepce. In 1939 the 'Magical Box' was invented that would be best known as the television in the years to come. The first television broadcast was Franklin D Roosevelt on NBC. After the first broadcast was sent off, the company

RCA began to sell televisions, and it became a huge hit. Since the TV was designed to look just like furniture, it was appealing to consumers and fit right in every living room. The first commercial arcade video game was created in 1971 and was called 'Computer Space'. It was produced by a company called Nutting Associates. Video games would eventually become one of the most popular mediums for telling simple stories in the 20th and 21st centuries. By presenting to the world a new way to be in a story, video games have made it possible for us to put ourselves in the shoes of a character and to embark on adventures and journeys as if they were real.

In this day and age, having a social media account means you have access to see everyone's life without actually being there. With social media, looking someone up on the internet has never been easier. The internet has created a space for blogs, posting pictures and events that you can attend to.

Although traditional ways of storytelling tells us about our histories, the contemporary methods such as the new generation of Virtual Reality (VR) add a social aspect to storytelling. However, in some ways, with the advent of VR in the modern era, we have circled back to visual storytelling as brands strive to find their narratives.

The evolution of storytelling reflects how people learn and communicate. Storytelling originated with visual stories, from cave drawings to oral storytelling to multimodal modes of storytelling. Though the mediums have changed, the core concept of using a sequence of events in an exciting narrative has remained the same. Today, social media has become the modern way we tell the stories of our lives and in the 21st century, social media is a time capsule for all humankind.

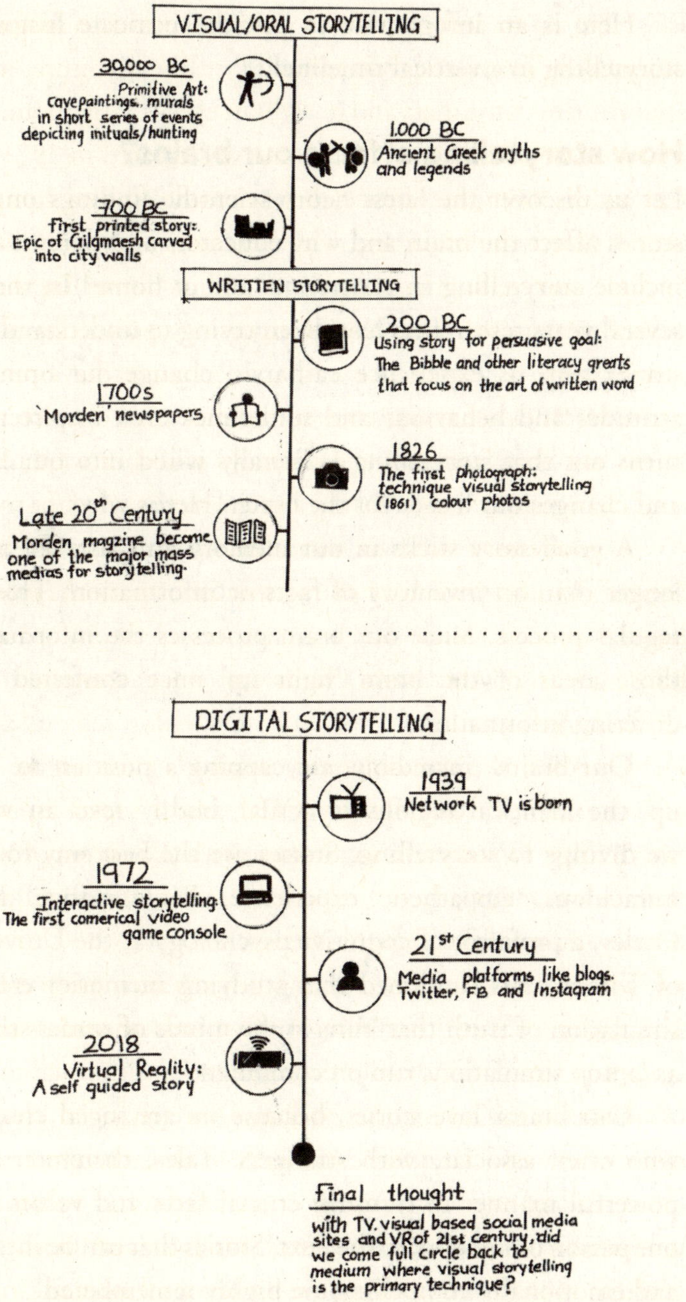
VISUAL/ORAL STORYTELLING
30,000 BC
Primitive Art: cavepaintings, murals in short series of events depicting rituals/hunting
1,000 BC
Ancient Greek myths and legends
700 BC
First printed story: Epic of Gilgmaesh carved into city walls
WRITTEN STORYTELLING
200 BC
Using story for persuasive goal: The Bibble and other literacy greats that focus on the art of written word
1700s
`Morden' newspapers
1826
The first photograph: technique visual storytelling (1861) colour photos
Late 20th Century
Morden magzine become one of the major mass medias for storytelling.
DIGITAL STORYTELLING
1939
Network TV is born
1972
Interactive storytelling: The first comerical video game console
21st Century
Media platforms like blogs, Twitter, FB and Instagram
2018
Virtual Reality: A self guided story
Final thought
with TV, visual based social media sites and VR of 21st century, did we come full circle back to medium where visual storytelling is the primary technique?

Here is an infographic to put the intricate history of storytelling in a vertical timeline!

How storytelling affects our brains?

Let us discover the latest neuro-scientific findings on how stories affect the brain and why educators and parents must include storytelling in classrooms and at home? In the last several years researchers have been trying to understand how stories help us experience catharsis, change our opinions, attitudes and behaviour and sometimes even inspire us. It turns out that storytelling is literally wired into our DNA and changes our brains for the better. Here's why?

A good story sticks in our memory and lasts for much longer than an inventory of facts or information. This is a regular process. Since our brain processes the information, those areas of the brain 'light up' once conferred with differing information.

Our brains, incredibly, are capping a position to 'light up' the identical regions of actual, bodily revel in whilst we divulge to storytelling. Stories are the best way for this miraculous, empathetic experience. For instance, Keith Oatley, a professor of cognitive psychology at the University of Toronto has cautioned that studying memories create a simulation of truth that 'runs at the minds of readers simply as laptop simulations run on computers.'

Our brains love stories, because we are social creatures who often associate with strangers. Tales, therefore, are a powerful manner to transmit crucial facts and values from one person or network to the next. Stories that can be intimate and emotionally compelling are highly remembered.

There are two main aspects for a story to be effective. First, it must attract and hold the attention of the listeners, in order for them to be curious. Secondly, it must be able to create a distance from our reality and transport us to the world of the characters.

From the perspective of story-telling, the audience is captivated if they experience excitement regarding the story being told. One attends to it because one has a tendency to perceive and find resolution. One's brain at the same time produces signs of arousal. One's central and respiratory systems speed up, stress hormones are discharged, and one's focus increases.

Once a story has sustained our attention long enough, we have a tendency to reciprocate emotions, which resonates with the characters. For instance, Bond trades blows with a villain on the prime of a dashing train. The intensity of the imagery transports the audience to the vividness of the scene. Transportation is a tremendous neural effort. One knows that one is watching fiction yet is being transported to it through their emotion.

Stories bring brains together

Emotional stimulation is the inspiration for fellow feeling. That is strong for social creatures like human beings as it allows us to envision the near future. When a person experiences several emotions together, the neural mechanism enables them to maintain balance or take quick action (Paul J. Zak, Ph.D. 2015).

A doctor's laboratory pioneered the behavioural study of endocrine, which is known to endorse fellow feeling and narrative transportation. It is established that once the brain synthesizes endocrine, individuals become trusting, generous, charitable, and compassionate. We know from the doctor's statement that the endocrine makes us highly sensitive to social cues around us which encourage us to interact and to assist others. However, it is only helpful if the recipient is open to such an interaction.

New analysis has known neurons within the brain. That 'light up' to the sound of singing however, doesn't reply to other styles of music. The work provides proof for comparatively fine-grained segregation of performing at intervals. Those are the auditory area, during an exceedingly approach that aligns with an intuitive distinction at intervals the music.

Neural Activity

Neural Coupling: When one is listening to, reading or watching a story, a part of the brain activates and allows us to resonate with the characters in the story.

Psychologists refer to this as 'flight of imagination as narrative transport'. It occurs when we are fully occupied with a story. It is understood that the greater the level of empathy in the reader/listener, the deeper is the experience of transportation. The brain however, engages itself in the story.

Children who are four to five years old usually develop the theory of mind, which makes them able to put themselves in another person's shoes to develop awareness.

Mirroring: When listening, reading or watching a story the brain performs a similar activity with those who are occupied with the story, be it the audience or the storyteller.

Storytelling therefore, breeds compassion.

Cortex Activity and hormones: When one gets engrossed in a story, it activates several parts of the brain, which enables the brain to comprehend more complex emotions and information. An activated brain means a more engaged heart.

'Emotions triumph Logic.'

Listening to a story that is being told or read to you activates the auditory cortex of the brain. Engaging with the story also fires up the left temporal cortex of the brain which is receptive to language. The cortex is capable of filtering out overused words. That is why the most skilled storytellers are extremely careful about the language they use. While doing so, they employ a host of literally techniques to keep the brain engaged.

Once, it is engaged, soon other regions of the brain begin to participate in the process. An instance of this would be the connections and the emotions we may feel with a story. A well told story also stimulates the frontal and the parietal lobes of our brains.

Powerful descriptions of food such as 'yummy yummy in my tummy, mouth-watering, juicy watermelon' will also stir

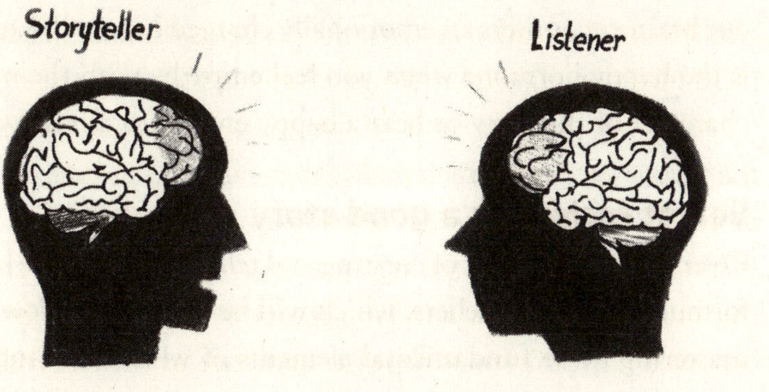

up the sensory cortex, while description of motion or action will get a response from the sensory motor region of the brain. Just thinking about running can activate the neurons associated with the physical act.

Research shows brain activity after listening to a story can last for several days, explaining why good stories tend to stay with us. Stories also improve the ability to recall any information embedded. Recalling a story is better than recalling facts.

Mental activity can bring about changes in the body. During an action scene or tension, the stress hormone cortisol is released into the bloodstream, which leads to greater immersion and response to the story. Some storytellers like to call this the cliffhanger. The more the listeners are kept on the cliffhanger, the higher the release of cortisol.

Character driven stories will affect the release of oxytocin into the blood, that is an empathy hormone that helps people bond. In fact, it is the same hormone that is released into the bloodstream of breastfeeding mothers.

Amygdala, an almond shaped structure in the limbic system of the brain is the key to how we process strong emotions like fear and pleasure. Dopamine is released when our brain encounters an emotionally charged event. Oxytocin is the happy hormone when you feel empathy with the main character of the story or hear a happy ending to the story.

Secret recipe for a good story

Over the years, the art of creating and telling a story have been formulated by storytellers, which will be discussed below. By mastering these fundamental elements of what constitutes a story, you can turn your concept into a gripping tale. These elements are theme, characters, setting, plot, conflict, point of view, and style.

Theme of the story: A good theme will elevate the story and help it create an everlasting impact on the listeners. Instead of spelling out the theme, different techniques and methods such as foreshadowing can be used for the listeners to discover it on their own.

Characters of the story: Characters make your story comprehensive. Their personalities and interactions with one another naturally create conflict and steer the story forward. Well-crafted characters will make the story more relevant. When listeners begin to imagine them in the characters' shoes and recognize the aspects of the characters' personalities in people they know, they develop a stronger connection with the story as a whole.

Setting or the background story: The setting is the world in which the story will take place, which includes locations and time. As we proceed into the story gradually, it allows the listener to create a mental picture of the fictional world as the story unfolds, making a more immersive experience.

Plot of the story: The plot is the main element of a story, which is characterized by events taking place in the story. As the story progresses, the protagonist encounters the inevitable climax. The pattern of 'cause and effect' induces a sense of conspiracy and suspense, leaving the audience curious.

Conflict: The underlying tension in the story is conflict. Whether its source is external or internal for the protagonist, it is the most important element of the story. Conflict creates tension by giving the protagonist some sense of purpose. It gets the listener more invested in the story.

Point of view: The point of view of a story is the perspective from which it is told. However, the listener may interpret it in different ways.

Style: The narrating or writing style is the culmination of all the characteristics that make your storytelling unique. Style of the story is crucial, from its momentum to its tone to the diction used in the story.

In order to master the art of storytelling, whether oral or written, one must bear these seven significant elements in one's mind.

Story Arc or Story Mountain

The human brain 'needs' meaning. We need to understand 'why' things happen in a certain way, why we cannot avoid it or 'why' things are well in order for us to continue with our activities. Therefore, the human brain loves a good story, because stories give us a sense of meaning, purpose and shape and good storytellers do that through knowledge of how stories must be developed, their arcs, etc.

Stories are inclined to follow a universal structure, popularly known as a story arc or story mountain. In the 19th century, German novelist Gustav Freytag described story arc through the following elements:

- **Exposition** is to set the scene. The characters and setting are introduced, providing a powerful description and background.
- **Inciting Incident** sets off the action in the story. A single event usually signals the commencement of the main conflict.

- **Rising Action** builds the story and makes it more exciting.
- **Climax** is the moment of utmost tension in a story and is often the most exciting event. It is the event that the rising action builds up to and that the falling action follows.
- **Falling Action** happens as a result of the climax, and which indicate that the story is coming to an end soon.
- **Resolution** is the central problem or conflict that the main character solves or is solved by someone else for him or her.
- **Dénouement** is the ending. At this point, any remaining questions or mysteries which remain after the resolution are solved by the characters.

Story arc provides a backbone to the story by providing a clear beginning, middle and end to it.

How does Storytelling Affect the brain

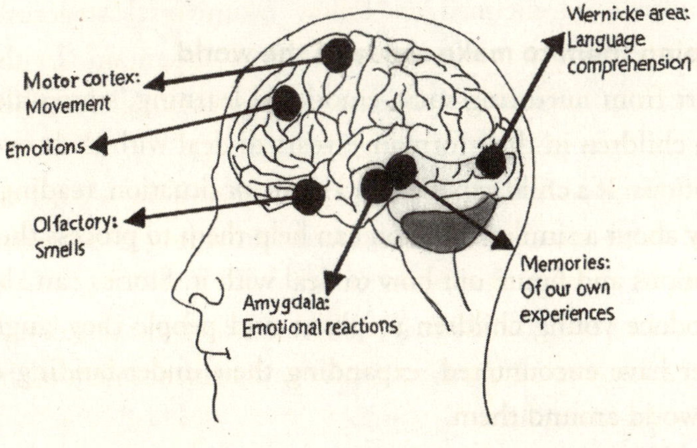

Benefits of telling stories to young children

We are all partial to a good story and children are some of the keenest storytellers around! Children love stories, whether they are telling them or listening to them. While, they are a fun way for leisure, they are also integral for the development of skills in a child. They can shape the way children view the world and even influence their personalities. Hence, it is essential to introduce children to stories in various formats and themes.

Some of the major benefits of storytelling for children are:

Increasing socio-emotional awareness

Research has shown that listening to stories can help young children to develop their social and emotional awareness, becoming more empathetic and enable them to understand the emotions of others. This means that young children are more equipped to recognize different emotions, making them better at predicting emotional responses. This contributes in developing their socio-emotional skills, helping them to intermingle more positively with others.

Helping them to make sense of the world

Apart from nurturing socio-emotional learning, stories also help children in their formative years to deal with their own emotions. If a child experiences a difficult situation, reading a story about a similar situation can help them to process their emotions and figure out how to deal with it. Stories can also introduce young children to places and people they might never have encountered, expanding their understanding of the world around them.

Developing literacy skills

Listening to stories help a child increase his or her literacy skills, even if the story is not enclosed in a story book. Asking questions about the story can help to build reading and comprehension skills. It also provokes critical thinking abilities in children. Moreover, asking open ended questions such as 'how did this happen?' or 'what do you think the character was thinking?' can help children to understand better.

Making Childhood Connections

Stories play a huge role in shaping the social interactions of a child. By the time children are in their second year they begin to understand basic concepts.

This changes as soon as a child begins to develop narrative skills. It will give them a better mechanism for making sense of the world around them. By the age of four or five a child develops empathy and awareness thus, enabling them to build better connections with the world around them.

Tips for great storytelling

Telling stories to young children is a good way to enhance their language, social and emotional skills, but it is often challenging to know which stories to tell, and how to tell them in an engaging way. Here are some tips on storytelling.

Tell stories you love: Stories you tell could be from books or your memory, what matters is your enthusiasm! Whether you want to tell your children about the time you found a rare shell on the beach, or a scary story. It is your love for stories which keeps children engaged.

Choose a story that incorporates shared interests. For example, if you and your children love pets, you may decide to tell a story about a heroic dog rescue. If you and your child share a mutual love for sports, your story can be about a world cup victory. Whichever story you select, make sure you ask lots of questions as you proceed through its plot, which ensures the children's undivided attention.

Use props: Props add a whole new element and a lot of fun to a story. They help children to visualize the characters and the setting of the story more effectively. Bring your safari tale to life with some hats and khaki—they add adventure to create an extra layer of engagement. For toddlers, consider creating a story box which contains several small objects that could be incorporated into your story. Children love to play. Therefore, using props such as small dolls, puppets and action figures might help them to grasp complex concepts and keep them engaged. They also help them remember the story more effectively. You could create simple drawings or finger puppets and then build stories around them.

Be expressive: When telling stories, storytellers often use facial expressions, body language and gestures that match the mood of the story. It is crucial to make sure the voice and body language are clearly expressing the tone and the emotions of the story. Body language aids in painting a picture in the listener's brain about the non-verbal events taking place in a scene along with all the senses. Good storytellers often talk about an event with a frown on their face, the raising of an eyebrow or a cold stare. This helps children understand what the settings are like, how the characters are feeling and how they should be feeling at a certain point in the tale. You practice body language by choosing a simple physical action, such as walking across the room and how it would vary across different scenarios. For instance, how would you walk if you were in a hot desert? Or if you were coming home after a long day at work and you know you have chores to do?

Modulate your voice as the characters demand. It prevents the storyteller from sounding monotonous. Each character should have their own unique voice, for the listener to be more immersed in the story. In fact, it is not the visual props but the appropriate sound of a character which makes its lively. However, it is not as easy as it sounds. Some people find adding expression to their voices trickier than others. But with the correct methods and techniques, you can master the art of modulating your voice. As for instance, you may try saying the sentence 'Where are you going?' in different ways. You may begin by saying it casually, as if you are watching your favourite show. When your child walks in, you may try to sound suspicious, angry, panicky or happy. Keep trying until you are comfortable with expressing a range of emotions in your voice.

Have an eye contact: Making an eye contact is an important storytelling skill. Through eye contact you can connect to the audience. Each child will feel as if the story is especially told to him/her. The most vital element to successful eye contact is to tell your story with soft eyes to the children in the room one by one. You can reach out to each child and monitor the reaction of children—whether they are enjoying your story or not.

Use dramatic pauses: People usually speak more quickly than the brain can process. A dramatic pause is used to foreshadow the scenes. For instance, when you ask a question if it is known what has happened. Pausing at crucial moments within the story heightens tension in the narrative and gets the audience involved. Children also get a prospect to critically think about the piece of information given during the story.

Structure your story: It essential that your story has a recognizable structure. The simplest way to do this is to make sure that the story is being told well and can be easily remembered. If you are choosing a new story, make sure you are prepared to embark it upon with an audience. Read it at least twice or thrice to make sure you are familiar with the settings, plot and characters. Each and every part of the story is important when you compose your plotline, be it a fictional story for a concept or a non-fictive narration. Although the story should revolve around the central idea, you have to make sure that every part of the story is crucial to the ending.

The pace and narrative of a story must be able to hold the attention of the listeners. Children in this case, must be presented with a story styled such that, it encourages them to listen. You must be able to use this plan of action in any lesson. Once you have done that, you might want to do something like a story arc, which helps you to map the key events and plot of a story, so that you remember it better. This also makes an outstanding comprehension activity after the story and it will assess whether your storytelling was successful!

Keep the story and its language simple: Some psychologists argue that telling stories is one of the first ways that allow humans to learn. Even if you are teaching science or math ideas, try to put a word or two that your children might not have come across earlier at the centre of the session. Describe and outline the word first and use it throughout the story. Since the audience is young, easy is apparent. However, even older audiences may be deeply compact after you take an ornate plan and cut back it to a hunk that they will remember.

Stories to have an important take away point: The end of a story is more effective, and your children will remember no matter what story scenario you paint. It adds depth and will make a story more memorable.

Practice your story well: You can go out of your way to learn new stories, and take gratification in creating your own. But if you want to get better at it, you have to practice it! What approach you take in telling your stories, always remember the most significant aspect of storytelling is the pleasure that comes with it. True storytellers love stories, so as long as you take pleasure in what you are doing, you cannot go wrong with it!

Scientists say stories are how our brains learn the best. They have a profound affect and shape our brains. They are the most effective teaching tool that we have as they connect the brain and the heart. The adventures of story characters that children experience through listening or reading stories are almost certain to have a lifelong impact.

This is a crucial time in their development, not just in terms of vocabulary or reading skills, but in the broader terms of their ability to think, empathize and imagine. So, educators and parents are encouraged to create happy memories and experiences through storytelling to ensure a strong and sure start!

Abigail Carr

Parent Coach, and University Lecturer at Hong Kong Baptist University

Abigail has 25 years of specialisation in teaching Early Childhood Education and Care. She works closely with parents to take them from being anxious, overwhelmed, and unsure about their child's behaviour, development, and educational learning to clear, connected, and trusting of the processes by which they can positively influence their child's moral character and academic outcomes, without stress. She has designed her parent education and coaching programs to provide parents with the knowledge, skills, and attitudes to support and improve behaviour and learning outcomes.

TWO

DEVELOPMENT OF THE 'ECOLOGICAL-SELF'

IN THE last fifty years the natural world has been pushed to its limits as humans produce and consume food and energy with what seems like a blatant disregard for the planet. The world is heating up, extreme natural disasters like fires and floods occur year after year across the globe, and the number of wild animals is reducing rapidly. The WWF (2020) speculates that Covid-19 itself is 'a manifestation of our broken relationship with nature' but that it also highlights the deep interconnection between people and the planet. It is both this natural interconnection and the perceived broken link between humans and the natural world that brings me to write this chapter.

Parents, caregivers and educators have a special kind of influence to empower children to make a change in the world. We need to nurture a generation of humans that want to, and can, break the cycle of waste production and the general indifference towards the planet and everything that is a part of it, including us humans. We need future leaders and decision-makers who will put nature as the top priority and also, innovation to build infrastructure which is effective in the fight for climate justice, rather than increasing our profits.

The aim is to understand how we can truly and intrinsically, empower the next generation to care about the Earth, so they can define its and their own future.

Reviewing Theory and Research

Anthropocentrism vs Ecocentrism

There is an argument against anthropocentrism, the belief that humans are the central and most important entity in the universe and that human well-being should prevail against all else. This in itself has been proposed by some to be the root cause of the world's environmental problems (White 1967). Grey (1993) challenged this, and proposed that the problem has not been with anthropocentrism and the concern for human wellbeing, but in shallow human-centredness, or 'shallow ecology' (Naess in Ims 2015). Shallow ecology is defined as when humans do not make the distinction that the 'non-human world' has independent value in itself, and people do not extend their moral standing to things and beings other than humans (Jakobsen 2007, Abram 1997). In fact, to live in harmony with the natural world, one has to consider what constitutes human well-being, and to look at their needs in corelation to those of our planet.

Anthropocentric ethics hold that humans have some responsibilities regarding the natural world but not direct responsibilities for the natural world—we are not responsible for the entirety of our actions on the planet, but to focus on how they affect us, our well-being and our quality of life (Jakobsen, 2007). On the other hand, eco-centric individuals value nature for its own sake and claims that it deserves protection because of its own unique and intrinsic value. For Grey (1993) there is a middle ground where enriched and open-minded anthropocentrism can provide the means for a reasonable ethical obligation and concern for all in the world that is not human. Having the concern and feeling of obligation, although important, does not however, equate with action and making changes. Notably, Gagnon Thompson and Barton (1994) found that those who are more ecocentric are much more likely to act on their pro-environment attitudes and engage in conserving behaviours compared to those with open-minded anthropocentric views.

Arne Naess, a Norwegian philosopher, conceived the 'deep ecology movement,' and highlighted the difference between deep and shallow ecological thinking—how we think about our interconnectedness with nature. Do we see ourselves as a part of it, or has our very humanness, with our complex brain structure and high intelligence, separated us from it? Do we stand on the outside looking in to what we compartmentalise as 'nature', or do we stand with and as a part of it? Though Naess keenly looked at the science of ecology, it was the philosophical thinking behind ethical questions that humans can ask about how we live, that prompted him to suggest that every person should think deeply about their own ecosophy—their philosophy of ecological harmony, and their approaches to living better (Ims 2015).

Devall and Sessions (1985 cited in Luke 2002 p180) elaborated on what they saw to be the central notion of the 'deep ecology' approach—'the basic intuitions and experiencing of ourselves and Nature, which comprise ecological consciousness'. Ecological consciousness is a person's relationship with nature, and the mindfulness by which they mediate their behaviour in the 'natural world,' and how they express the value that they put onto nature. Studies show that this type of environmental consciousness is a 'complex mental education,' which includes cognitive, regulatory, emotional and ethical aspects (Panov 2013). This chapter attempts to consider these aspects with regards to early childhood development and education, because, as Biriukova (2005) pointed out, re-shaping adults' attitudes towards the natural world and towards ecological consciousness is challenging and to do so in a short amount of time would be near impossible. Children on the other hand, particularly those under six years old, are at a stage where they are not burdened by anthropocentric attitudes and are inclined to internalize meaning and understanding. This can set the foundation of their understanding about the world and themselves. The early years is a key period to be ensuring that we encourage the development of children's relationship with nature.

Research has shown that in the development of children's biological reasoning, or how they make sense of biological phenomenon, anthropocentrism is most likely an acquired perspective and not something they are born with. Herrmann et al. (2010), made comparisons of five-year-old rural children and five-year-old urban children in their US study. They found that those who grew up in urban areas were more likely to privilege human over non-human form, perhaps pertaining to their lesser experience around non-human forms. Though most pertinently, they also found that three-year-olds in both the urban and rural groups did not appear to privilege humans, concluding that anthropocentric reasoning may not be an obligatory step in development, but rather one that is likely learnt by urban children between three and five years old. The role of the parents and caregivers, as well as the cultural connotations for this were explored in Waxman and Medin's study (2007). From their findings, they discussed how urban children are not destined for an anthropocentric view of the world, but they are sensitive to the discourse of the adults in their community, as well as the culturally prevalent models of anthropocentrism that they might experience.

We know that during the early years, children's brains go through a major stage of synaptic development. It is during this time where the capacity of the limbic system and self-awareness (emotional, behavioural and long-term memory function) is expanded (Brown and Jernigan 2012, Trevarthen & Delafield-Butt 2017). It appears extremely important that we not only provide deep and meaningful experiences, but also stay hyper-aware of how and what we do and say ourselves, will influence young children during this time of rapid growth and development. In fact, we can (and should) strategically look into how the development of ecological consciousness may be simpler and easier within the younger generation, and therefore, we should maximise their experiences and understanding of themselves in and of the natural world. If we mitigate strong anthropocentric views from forming at all, perhaps then, they will be keenly positioned for taking an ecocentric approach to how they interact with, and as a part of, the natural world as they grow up.

Taking a deeper look into the development of 'self', and self in relation to the natural world, ecology and ecocentrism, may give us a wider view of what that may mean for how we perceive our own responsibilities for young children's exposure to the environment and nature. As with all psychological approaches, theories and concepts, this line of investigation may enlighten us to how we can raise children and run programmes that develop a deep-rooted obligation to the environment. To provide a foundation for understanding the characteristics of human awareness and responsiveness to and with nature, we should also take a look at how ecological consciousness is formed, in order for us to see what we can do to support its development in young children.

The Formation of Ecological Consciousness

Consciousness itself is a defining feature of human life and experience. Miroshkin et al. (2019 p596) describe its formation as a result of an individual's 'psyche change'; when a person's perception, experience and behaviour are integrated into a state of mind, or an emotional and behavioural way of functioning. These states of mind then become the mechanisms for awareness of our existence and are especially useful for enabling behaviour (Baumeister et al 2011). In terms of ecological consciousness, this transcends to more than just an awareness of nature, but the acknowledgement and understanding of humans as biological beings and an intricate part of the web of life.

Trevarthen and Delafield-Butt (2017 p5) discuss that consciousness begins in-utero before birth and the interactions that infants experience upon being born develop 'affective consciousness' of sensations and feelings within the body, that extend to awareness of the outside world through the senses. Over time, this culminates in the development of self-awareness and the sense of self that is discussed in depth in psychological study. The development of the self is widely thought to be affected by the socio-cultural environment of a child. How they experience attachments with caregivers and how they are encouraged to explore the world around them, impacts how they see and understand themselves within the wider community and environment as they grow older (Bretherton 1992). It also affects how they view their place in the world and their connection to different aspects of their experiences of it. It impacts their potential for learning and becoming, or the development of their 'self-realisation'.

Tonnesvang (2006 p54) described self-realisation as 'finding a unique, personal style in one's way of discovering, living, and fulfilling oneself'. As a psychological, philosophical and spiritual concept, we can simplify our understanding of self-realisation as one's identity, what one stands for and a deep understanding of oneself that allows us to make decisions and act in relation to our environment. It is generally thought to be a work in progress throughout a lifetime and the process by which we make our lives meaningful (Brooke 2009). For Naess (1987 p35), when describing his interpretation of self-realisation, he considered that our view of 'self' as the 'ego', and the psychological understanding of the development of the social self (learnt through our social roles and experiences), is far too narrow. We largely leave out nature in human development and psychology, despite the fact that we exist as living beings on Earth. So, he introduced the concept of the 'ecological-self' (eco-self) which means 'to be in, of and for nature from our very beginning'.

Does this then, further invite us to reconsider the experiences we provide our very youngest children, at a critical time when they develop their conscious understanding of who they are, where they are from and what meaning they attribute to how they want to live their life? Naess' deep ecology movement and the development of the eco-self, calls upon a shift to support one's natural inclinations towards nature. He believed that we should move away from a view of moral obligations about how to treat and use nature appropriately, which can feel like sacrifices for moral good. He suggested that only a change in our own view of nature itself can promote an ethical transformation. We need to move away from a mainly scientific focus on nature that exacerbates.

The Ecological-Self (Eco-self)

The gap we wedge between us and the natural world, as if we are not a part of it, to the deep philosophical reflections on our reality as humans, as nature and Earth itself (Cavazza 2014).

The word 'eco' comes from the Greek word 'oikos', meaning 'household', i.e., natural habitat. The eco-self is, in simple terms, our identification with the world around us (our home). For example, to identify with a tree, not because we believe we are identical to a tree of course, but to recognise our commonalities (Strumse 2007). It feels beneficial here to look first at the developmental theories of the 'Self' in order to further consider our understanding of the development of the eco-self.

Behavioural psychological theories would suggest that the self is developed through learned responses to stimuli, which can be from observing others or from conditioning. For example, learning how a female 'should' behave as a girl through the experiences that others have bestowed upon them over and again. I play with pink dolls therefore, I am a girl or I am a girl, so I should play with pink dolls, for example. This links closely with the sociological approaches to the self, that tries to understand the influence of social obligations on development, at both a macro and a micro-level. For sociologists, the development of the self is in the triadic nature of our individual experiences interacting with our inner world when with others, and also with the environment.

According to the sociologist Cooley (1902), the self is defined as a collection of beliefs that we hold, and is developed through a process of interaction with the social environment. Mead (1934) elaborated on this proposing that the individual is not passive in the development of the self, they play an active role. The effect a person has on the process of their own socialisation (i.e., how active a part they take in it themselves) as well as the other people involved in the process (family & friends for example) impacts how the self develops. If we take the example of the pink dolls from above, the active role the child takes in accepting and playing with pink dolls would impact the way they would experience this part of their self-development. If they show no interest in the dolls people will likely to stop giving them. Therefore, they play an active role in halting the process of self-development in relation to being a female human and playing with pink dolls. If they show interest, talk about the doll, play with the doll, ask for another doll, people may give them more dolls, and more pink things too. Therefore, they play an active role in the way their social environment has impacted their sense of self in relation to being a human female.

In psychoanalytic theories of development such as those proposed by Freud and Erikson, the 'Self' is developed in the unconscious mind, lodged there from past experiences, and a person takes a passive role in its development of the ego. The ego is the conscious part of the self that for Freud plays the lesser role, than do the unconscious parts i.e., the Id and the Superego. It is the ego that needs to control the innate and primal urges of the unconscious (Boyd and Bee 2009). For Erikson the development of the ego or the self, happens constantly throughout our lives. The self, or a person's identity, goes through stages of crisis in order to reach mastery and full competence at each stage of development. For example, in the toddler years the 'self' experiences the crisis of autonomy vs shame and doubt, where children master physical autonomy over toilet training and other traits of independence. If they fail, for Erikson, they will experience internalised shame and doubt that will stay a part of their identity and personality, their 'self' (Boyd and Bee 2009).

It feels appropriate at this point to remark on another psychoanalytic theorist who is known for also branching into philosophical thinking. Although he had his fair share of critiques, Carl Jung throws a little light on the link between the self, ecology and the natural world. Jung, like Freud and

Erikson, theorised about the ego and consciousness. From a Jungian perspective, the development of the self is a life-long process of integrating the ego (a person's consciousness) with the unconscious, which includes 'the personal unconscious' (everything that one knows but is not actually thinking at a particular moment) and 'the collective unconscious' (the human blue-print or innate human instincts) (Journal Psyche accessed 2022). The aim of self-development for Jung, is to reach self-realisation through actualising the entirety of one's potential, and this can take a lifetime.

Jung was known for suggesting that humans must look closer at how the self develops from its original or most primitive form (Brooke 2009). Highlighted the major shift we have taken, especially since significant advances in technology, away from where we evolved—i.e., the Earth—towards what we can (and want to) gain, build or materialise into our outer world. He considered that we have become materialistic and do not acknowledge our primal human instincts (self-preservation, sexual and social) in a way that helps us understand our inner world or psyche, and how we react and interact with the outer world as a human. (Journal Psyche 2018). Jung appears to suggest that, as we are from and of nature, our unconscious holds the link back to it, within ourselves and our psyche.

The works of radical empiricist and realist James Gibson who founded ecological psychology, highlighted what he believed to be a key physiological link between the environment and humans (Chawla 2007). Proposing that the environment and animals (including humans), are not separable items (Reed 1996), Gibson's work challenged the realm of cognitive psychology, where it is believed that a person's internal, mental world processes the 'meaningless' external world, to make meaning and support development. Gibson (1966) provided the notion that our sensory systems are integrated with cognitive processes. He proposed that we experience our surrounding physical environments through stimuli in our senses, i.e., the very nature of the terrain of the ground, and the way that particles move in air, and how light moves and refracts, has impacted the evolution of our sensory-motor systems. This, by immediate relation, has affected the cognitive processes they are integrated with, including the development of self and self-awareness.

Gibson's work looks closer at the actual interconnection of human beings as part of nature and the direct link of the environment to our psychological development. However, ecological psychology is not in mainstream studies. Although other ecological systems models, such as that theorised by Bronfenbrenner touch on the different levels of influence from the environment (family, peers, school, work and culture) on child development, even these do not look deeply at the impact of the non-human world on human development. It appears that, unfortunately, psychology has generally left a large void around where and how the interconnection with the non-human world fits in our development of 'self'.

It appears to be in philosophical thought that the link emerges more obviously. Interestingly, according to the Buddhist view, the essence of the self actually does not exist at all. It is suggested that it is the egotism that comes with the belief in a 'self' that contributes to human's view of themselves as unrestricted users of the world's resources. This results in the anthropocentrism that can naturally develop in childhood. For Buddhists, the idea is that of the 'no-self'. It comes from the understanding that humans cannot ever be just one 'self', as we are always a new version of ourselves and therefore, the 'I'-self is deceptive (Wang 2016). Our constant interactions with the world change us every second, psychologically and physiologically and therefore the ego that we cling to in fact does not, and should not, exist. This is not the non-existence of the physical self, for which the semantics of using 'I' and 'me' in language is accepted, but rather it is the 'loss of self-preoccupation'. With a loss of self-preoccupation, could we naturally bring our thoughts and actions back into a state of 'at oneness' with the Earth?

It is logical from here to circle back to Naess' philosophical deep ecology movement, where he also maintained that self-realisation goes beyond egoistic identification and towards a wider sense of identification with the non-human world (Schroll 2007), the eco-self. So, let us now look at the practicalities of what we can do and how we can encourage, support and maintain this deeply ecological and non-egoistic identification with the world in young children.

Practical Applications

Developing a Parental Ecosophy

Parents are the early guides for children's values and moral development. They make decisions about their child's lifestyles, and where and how they spend their time. They model behaviour, language and thought processes, and generally lay the foundations to live. Children's early brain development sets them up to develop a strong eco-self, but without a sturdy family focus on it, strong anthropocentric values might easily take over as they reach middle childhood. There is a reason that young children may be able to name all the train stops on the map of the transit railway lines, or a teenager can describe what the latest top celebrity did at the weekend, but they can't easily name indigenous local flora and fauna. They perhaps have no desire to know much about the tree that provides them shade, as they sit looking at a mobile phone underneath it. It is the habits, ways of living and family traditions that they experience have a profound impact on their interests and focus as they mature.

Ask most parents how they would like their child to grow up, and they will say that they want them to be happy, successful and fulfilled. There is something in the desires of parents that makes them, as De Beyer (2012 p15) puts it, already committed to the future, through their visions for their child, making them a potentially 'powerful force of change'. Re-evaluating this view of what life fulfilment really looks like, particularly if focus on what the Earth could very well be, in the near future, and their children (and their children's children), is essential. We have already established that it is easier for us to support the development of the eco-self in young children, as opposed to in adults. Hence, the belief systems of the adults raising children also need careful examination and questioning.

Reassessing the visions parents have for their child's future values and morals to include an ecocentric and interconnectedness with the rest of the living world will require deep reflection, and the development of a family ecosophy or ecological philosophy. De Beyer (2012 p9) provides a suggested list of adjusted values parents may emphasise to mitigate the extractive culture that most humans live in and with today. A more ecocentric vision would see humility, egoless[ness], selflessness, standing back, [being] humble, kind, cooperative, non-competitive, giving things away (rather than taking and holding on), surrendering, open and receptive, ecological, contributory, inclusive, patient, [and] slow. Some philosophical questions that parents could ask themselves in establishing their ecosophy and visions for such values and morals could be:

- Does the future we can expect on Earth look like the future I want for my child's (and their children's) health and happiness?
- How do I want my grandchildren to experience the Earth if and when they arrive in this world?
- What can my child do today or in their future to help achieve that?
- What do I hope my child will leave behind when they die?
- In what way can they make the world a better place?
- What do I think a better world looks like?

Developing a family ecosophy a part of the programme of parent partnership in early years settings would be ideal to reach a wider parent audience for this. By encouraging parents' deeper thought about the connections to nature they provide for their children, and focusing on more than academic achievements for school, one may anticipate an extension towards children's harmonious interactions with the world as they grow older. Rather than just playing in nature together, open ended questions with the child, the family and staff of a setting should be reflected upon before, during and after the interaction with environment. The aim would be to bring an awareness about their connection with nature, how it makes them feel and what they would like to experience in the future.

In the long term, parents' contemplation on whether their child can truly be happy, successful and fulfilled without connecting to the non-human world is vital. Perhaps the aim for the self-realisation of children belonging to and becoming a part of nature itself, is the key to how the Earth, their home, might fare.

Philosophical Thinking and Conceptual Development

The ancient debate about whether children should 'do' philosophy, centres around the issues of acknowledging what philosophy actually is. Is it studying the world's great philosophical thinkers, or questioning life, and everything in it (Murris 2000)? Though both may be viewed as important for philosophical thinking over a lifetime, when we look from the point of view of early childhood education and development, we can focus on children's questioning and examining phenomena, with interest and critical thinking.

There are trains of thought that suggest children cannot truly philosophise. Though of course, they are concerned about meaning in a concrete way as they explore and question the world around them. Piaget suggested, in the preschool years, children are in the concrete operational stage of learning and understanding the world, they do not hypothesise and cannot think abstractly (Kitchener 1990).

But there is evidence that despite their young age and early cognitive development, even children in the preschool years are beginning to develop metacognition i.e., their ability to think and know about their own thoughts and knowledge (Kuhn 1999), or to think abstractly. It is likely that it is actually a very good time for them to experience philosophical questioning, as a way to deepen their ability to think. Formulating questions, and reflecting on concepts they know, concepts they do not know, and how they feel about their experiences related to particular concepts, will help them develop the building blocks of philosophical thinking. It is this later truly philosophical thought, that may have the bearing we need for how they approach the way they live as adults.

Questioning provides a practice in listening and understanding other people, but also the scope to listen to and understand the non-human world and develop their connection to it, particularly if practiced through a multisensory approach. During the preschool years a child becomes increasingly more aware of their own thoughts and they begin to know 'how' they know something, as well as what others might know and feel. It is during this time when we see more complex problem-solving take place, and with higher-order thinking practice they can enhance their metacognitive potential (Drigas et al 2021).

Kizel (2016) states that philosophy with children is all about their place in the world and it arises from the fresh questions that come to their minds. It is the role of the adult to provide the environment for this to happen, as well as step back and allow questions to form and flow. So how do we encourage philosophical thinking and questioning that supports the development of the eco-self? Firstly, we need to provide time and space for children to think and question and be open to all and every question they have. We want children to take an active part in their development of metacognition and deep thinking.

We can also guide thinking with our own questions, without inappropriately taking over children's train of thought. Some examples of philosophical questions we can ask young children could be:

- How do you feel here in the woods?
- What are you thinking about as you stand in the sea?
- What can you hear?
- What can you feel?
- If this tree could talk to you, what do you think it would say?
- How do you think this plant feels growing here next to the road?
- What would be something you would like to tell the grass under your feet?

Having some questions at our own fingertips is useful to guide children's thoughts, but we should also not be deterred by thinking that young children are not competent in language, and then assume that we should always guide them with our own questions. In fact, listening to children's 'why' questions and answering them with more questions is a fantastic way to support deep thinking. Even very young children and infants are often deep in thought as they touch, feel and sense objects and their environment. Without language they still think and, we should allow these processes the time and space they need to unfold.

It has been proposed that personal beliefs about knowledge and knowing, i.e., the metacognitive understanding we have discussed, has significant implications for the way people learn about and respond to social-ecological systems (Stave 2002, Fazey 2010). Building strong foundations in higher order thinking processes, making judgements and evaluating new information, appears to be essential for helping young children grow into deep-thinkers, problem-solvers and decision-makers (Pillow 2008). In the early years of course, we do not expect children to find solutions to prevent global warming, or clean up our oceans, though they may possibly have some great imaginative ideas for this. But what we can do to provide for the basis of this thinking, even for very young children and infants, is provide a place for children to have dialogue with adults and peers, and take part in shared discoveries, talking and questioning regularly as part of their play environment.

Siraj-Blatchford (2009) suggests that children should be scaffolded through constructivist discoveries in order to support all areas of learning but particularly their cognitive development and critical thinking skills. Through qualitative research, the term 'sustained shared thinking' ('SST') was coined. Others have used the term 'dialogic teaching' to mean the same thing – participation and interaction in thinking, to build understanding (Stibbard et al 2020). SST is not only for children who are able to use their verbal faculties, it can also and should, begin in infancy through emotional communication with caregivers and interactions with their environment. Smiling, cooing, back and forth interactions that will progress to object play together and then into symbolic play and then increasingly more structured activities (Siraj-Blatchford 2009). We want to provide these experiences and discoveries in and with nature as much as possible, to encourage the foundations of deep ecological understanding.

Flavell (2000) proposed that, although metacognition is a developmental process that continues until adulthood, even infants under one-year-old, begin to develop a 'theory of mind', meaning that they start to think about their mental states, such as desires and intentions and of others. Parents and educators naturally consider the importance of exposing infants and children to social experiences with other humans to strengthen and continue this development of understanding others. It is perhaps less common for us to contemplate the important 'eco-experiences' we can provide for them to develop an affinity with the non-human world too. As the theory of mind develops, the corresponding development of this connection with nature can grow alongside organically and intertwined with the development of empathy and self-regulation (and behaviour), not only when interacting with humans but also with the rest of the natural world.

Sensory Nature Engagements from Birth

With our understanding that human consciousness develops before birth and that the first sensory experiences that infants have when they come into the world will impact their developing consciousness, we should focus on enhancing early sensory engagement and explorations that babies have with the natural world. Learning takes places when the mind is able to put together information retrieved from all the senses. From the very moment a person is born, they learn how to interact with their environment using their senses of sight, listening, touch, smell, and taste, as well as their kinaesthetic and vestibular senses (spatial awareness, body positioning and balance). We know that the first three years of life are crucial for brain development, so in early years' settings, sensory play (play that stimulates one or more senses) is a regular occurrence, and a multi-sensory approach is usually used to support all areas of learning. This is because sensory memory stimulates neuropathways and synapse development in the brain when combined with emotion and attention i.e., through play, (Prendeville and Fearn 2016).

Here it is useful to remind ourselves again of Gibson's (1966), ecological psychology theory of perception i.e., us being aware through our senses, as well as to understand that the composition of our Earth (the terrain, the light, the air) along with the very evolution of ourselves as thinking beings, has catalysed how these senses function. Our cognitive abilities are a fascinating by-product. As David Abram (1997 p9) puts it 'the eyes, the skin, the tongue, ears, and nostrils—all are gates where our body receives the nourishment of otherness'; otherness for Abram being animate nature itself. In psychological and philosophical thought, the myriad sensory engagements humans have of and with nature are steeped in our deep physical and psychological connections with the Earth.

Since, it is our senses which result in our development—perhaps, we just need to take a glance at the ocean, the grass, or a forest to recognise their inherent sensory nature—we utilise the surroundings around us fore sensory play that our infants and children need. The trend for decorating early years indoor settings in natural earthy colours and using natural materials as much as possible, is often because of concerns of overstimulation. Upon reflection we might suppose that this very thought process highlights that nature provides the exact stimulus that infants and children need, without being too overpowering (Joseph Dou and Kemp 2022). It makes sense that our natural world would provide that for us.

In their study of English early childhood education settings Josephidou and Kemp (2022) used the Froebelian perspective of children as nature, to look at how infants experience natural environments. Friedrich Froebel, the German pedagogue laid the foundation for early childhood education and devised the name 'kindergarten' (children's garden) (Lilley 1976). With this, he reinforced the notion that children are nature. He used natural metaphors to describe child development, such as connecting it to the growth and nurturing of a flower. Froebel believed in the development of children's early experiences due to their interconnectedness with nature, but Josephidou and Kemp's study found that whilst outdoor experiences were planned for in settings, they were majorly focussed on what benefits nature was going to provide the children, rather than the important interconnections that can foster dispositions for a deep care for the Earth. They suggested that for under the age of two years, nature engaging pedagogy should include sleeping and sensory engagement with the elements whilst lying or sitting, to really be 'in and with nature', i.e., sleeping on the grass and sitting on the leaves. The literal physical, sensory connection we have to nature in our earliest years as we rapidly develop cognitively and in self-awareness, could be vital for the robust development of the eco-self.

There may be reservations for allowing infants and young children to touch, explore and physically connect with the non-human world, because our responsibility for safety is something we should not take lightly. But it is our attitude towards things that we can and are able to do, that will have the most bearing on the immersive experiences that children will have. It is really important to recognise that nature is all around us, it is the food we eat, the shade of the trees that line roads, the grass in our back gardens, the sky above our heads, the sun and stars that shine over us every day. Let us slow down, and acknowledge each and every form of nature as something we can immerse children in and encourage their physical and psychological connection to. This is an approach we surely can take hold of to support the development of our youngest humans and their interconnection with, and as a part of, nature.

Conclusion

Djernis et al. (2019) and Lim et al. (2020) found that for people to score higher on the Connectedness to Nature Scale, immersion was the most beneficial approach. They also found that alongside the physical health benefits of fresh air and sunlight, immersing oneself in nature has psychological benefits like improving mood and reducing depressive feelings and anxiety. With what we know about the plasticity of young brains, particularly in the first three years of life, imagine the powerful psychological and cognitive benefits for children growing up with nature immersion as naturally occurring experiences in their daily life. Perhaps we will see less depression and anxiety ingrained in our future societies, alongside a deeper respect for, and relationship with, the non-human world.

Neuro-science, psychology and philosophy allude to the importance of building a true connection with and to nature for our own health (physical and mental) and the Earth's. Ongoing and regular immersion of children with, as, and of nature, along with deep philosophical thought, and the development of critical thinking skills from the earliest years, are essential to developing a strong eco-self and for true ecological intent to come forth. For Machnev et al (2018) the development of ecological consciousness itself, requires purposeful activity and a system of norms and values. Therefore, a family ecosophy of nature immersion from birth would be highly beneficial to raising truly ecologically conscious individuals, and ones that identify themselves as a part of nature in their eco-self-image and eco-self-concept. The vastness, the serenity and the pureness of the natural world is alluring in itself, and in fact we are the ones that will miss out now, and in the future unless we mend our ways of living.

This chapter has attempted to look at the psychological and philosophical theory of the development of the eco-self. It provides an overall theoretical understanding of what 'eco-self' is and how its development contributes to the greater good of ecological harmony on our Earth. Every child in this world has a different experience of their family, community and nature-based life, but perhaps with a wider focus on the reality of their future happiness, success and feelings of fulfilment, the adults in their lives will do all they can to decrease self-preoccupation and enhance their earthly connectedness as natural beings of our planet, for them to be able to save it.

REFERENCES

Abram, David. *The Spell of the Sensuous.* New York: Vintage Books, 1997.

Roy, F. Baumeister, E. J. Masicampo and Katheleen D. Vohs. "Do Conscious Thoughts Cause Behavior?" *Annual Review of Psychology* 62, no. 1 (2011): 331–36.

Biriukova, N. A. "The Formation of an Ecological Consciousness." *Russian Education & Society* 47, no. 12 (2005): 34–35. https://doi.org/10.1080/10609393.2005.11056938

Boyd, Denise and Helen Bee. *Lifespan Development.* New York: Pearson, 2009.

Brooke, R. "The self, the psyche and the world: A phenomenological interpretation." *Journal of Analytical Psychology* 54, no. 5 (2009): 601–618.

Brown, T.T. and Jernigan, T. L. "Brain Development During the Preschool Years." *Neuropsychology Review* 22, no. 4 (2012): 313–333.

Bretherton, I. "The origins of attachment theory: John Bowlby and Mary Ainsworth". *Developmental Psychology* 28, no. 5 (1992): 759–775.

Cavazza, E. "Environmental Ethics as a Question of Environmental Ontology: Naess' Ecosophy T and Buddhist Traditions." *De Ethica, A Journal of Philosophical Theological and Applied Ethics* 1, no. 2 (2014): 23–48.

Chawla, L. "Childhood Experiences Associated with Care for the Natural World: A Theoretical Framework for Empirical results." *Children Youth and Environments* 17, no. 4 (2004): 144–170.

Cooley, C. H. "Looking-glass self." *Human Nature and the Social Order* (1902): 179–185.

De Beyer, M. "Raising Ecological Awareness." Msc. diss. Schumacher College, UK, 2012. https://megandebeyer.wordpress.com/2017/01/25/thethesis-ecological-awareness/.

Djernis, D., I. Lerstrup, D. Poulsen, U. Stigsdotter, J. Dahlgaard, and M. O'Toole. "A Systematic Review and Meta-Analysis of Nature-Based Mindfulness: Effects of Moving Mindfulness Training into an Outdoor Natural Setting." *International Journal of Environmental Research and Public Health* 16, no. 17 (2019): 3202.

Drigas, A., G. Kokkalia and A. Economou. "An 8-Layer Model for Metacognitive Skills in Kindergarten." *Neurology and Neurobiology* 4, no. 1 (2021): 2–10.

Fazey, I. "Resilience and higher order thinking." *Ecology and Society* 15, no. 3 (2010): 9–31.

Flavell. J.H. "Development of children's knowledge about the mental world International." *Journal of Behavioral Development* 24, no. 1 (2000): 15–23.

Gagnon, Thompson S. C. and M. A. Barton. "Ecocentric and anthropocentric attitudes toward the environment." *Journal of Environmental Psychology* 14, no. 2 (1994): 149–157.

Grey, W. "Anthropocentrism and deep ecology." *Australasian Journal of Philosophy* 71, no. 4 (1993): 463–475.

Herrmann, P., S. R. Waxman and D. L. Medin. "Anthropocentrism is not the first step in children's reasoning about the natural world." *Proceedings of the National Academy of Sciences* 107, no. 22 (2010): 9979–9984.

Ims, K. J. "Deep ecology and personal responsibility." In *The Spiritual Dimension of Business Ethics and Sustainability*, edited by L. Zsolnai. Switzerland: Springer International Publishing.

Jakobsen, T. G. "Environmental ethics: Anthropocentrism and non-anthropocentrism: Revised in the light of critical realism." *Journal of Critical Realism* 16, no. 2 (2017): 184–199.

Journal Psyche. "Jung and his Individuation Process." http://journalpsyche.org/jung-and-hisindividuation-process/.

Josephidou, J. and N. Kemp. "A life 'in and with nature?' Developing nature engaging and nature enhancing pedagogies for babies and toddlers." *Global Education Review* (2022): 1–33.

Kitchener, R.F. "Do children think philosophically?" *Metaphilosophy* 21, 40. 4 (1990): 416–431.

Kizel, A. "Philosophy with children as an educational platform for self-determined learning." *Cogent Education* 3 (2016): 1–11.

Kuhn, D. "A developmental model of critical thinking." *Educational Researcher* 28, no. 2 (1999): 16–46.

Lim, Pei Yi, Denise Dillon and Peter K. H. Chew. "A guide to nature immersion: Psychological and physiological benefits." *International Journal of Environmental Research and Public Health* 17, no. 16 (2020): 5989.

Luke, T. W. "Deep ecology living as if nature mattered: Devall and Sessions on defending the Earth." *Organization & Environment* 15, no. 2 (2002): 178–186.

Lilley. I. M. *Friedrich Froebel: A selection from his writings.* New York: Cambridge University Press, 1976.

Morris, C. W., ed. *Mind, Self, and Society*. Chicago: University of Chicago Press, 2015.

Miroshkin, D.V., A. V. Grinenko, M. M. Tkhugo, O. V. Mizonova, I. G. Kochetkov, S. N. Kazakova and N. G. Miloradova. "Psychology of ecological consciousness." *Ekoloji* 28, no. 107 (2019): 593–599.

Murris. K. "Can children do philosophy?" *Journal of Philosophy of Education* 34, no. 2 (2000): 261–279.

Naess, A. "Self-realization, An ecological approach to being in the world." *The Trumpeter* 4, no. 3 (1987): 35–42.

Panov, V. I. "Ecological thinking consciousness responsibility." *Procedia-Social and Behavioral Sciences* 86 (2013): 379–383.

Pillow, B. H. "Development of children's understanding of cognitive activities." *The Journal of Genetic Psychology* 169, no. 4 (2008): 297–321.

Prendeville, S. and M. Fearn. *Coming Alive, Finding Joy through Sensory Play in Creative Psychotherapy*. London: Routledge, 2016.

Reed E. S. *Encountering the World; Toward and Ecological Psychology*. New York: Oxford University Press, 1996.

Schroll, M. A. "Wrestling with Arne Naess: A chronicle of ecopsychology's origins." The Trumpeter 23, no. 1 (2007): 28–57.

Siraj-Blatchford, I. "Conceptualizing progression in the pedagogy of play and sustained shared thinking in early childhood education: A Vygotskian perspective." Education and Child Psychology 26, no. 2 (2009): 77–89.

Stave, K. A. "Using system dynamics to improve public participation in environmental decisions." *Systems Dynamics Review* 18, no. 2 (2002): 139–167.

Stibbard, A., C. Davidson and C. Edwards-Groves. "Changing talk and interaction for dialogic teaching in an Early Years' literacy classroom." *Journal of Teacher Action Research* 6, no. 3 (2020): 4–25.

Strumse, E. "The ecological self: A psychological perspective on anthropogenic environmental change." *European Journal of Science and Theology* 3, no. 2 (2007): 7–12.

Tønnesvang, J. "The structure of self-realization." *Journal of Theoretical and Philosophical Psychology* 26, no. 1–2 (2006): 51–77.

Trevarthen, C. and J. T. Delafield-Butt. "Development of consciousness." In *Cambridge Encyclopedia of Child Development*, edited by B. Hopkins, E. Geangu and S. Linkenauger, 821–835.

Waxman, S. and D. Medin. "Experience and Cultural Models Matter: Placing Firm Limits on Childhood Anthropocentrism." *Human Development* 50, no. 1 (2007): 23–30. http://dx.doi.org/10.1159/000097681

White, L. T. J. "The historical roots of our ecological crisis." *Science* 155, no. 3767 (1967): 1203–1207. Almond, R.E.A., M. Grooten and T. Petersen, eds. *Living Planet Report 2020 - Bending the Curve of Biodiversity Loss.* Gland: WWF, 2020.

LIDIA TAVANI
Anthropologist and Pedagogist specialised in Outdoor Education, Italy

Lidia has worked in Italian schools for more than 15 years – both in early childhood and primary – carrying out health education and natural environment awareness projects. She has worked in training others as outdoor educator and is associated with, 'Rete Scuole all'Aperto,' to implement outdoor curricula at public schools in Italy, especially those in urban areas. Lidia designs educational environments, both inside and outside. The most important outdoor project to date has been 'Laboratori all'aperto' ('Outdoor Labs'), designed for an Italian school in Rome.

THREE

THE OUTDOOR EDUCATION APPROACH

IN RECENT years in the world of education we have seen a growing interest in outdoor environments. Although this is still not a global interest, we note that more and more schools and early childhood centres are promoting outdoor activities—in their gardens and in green or urban areas. In most cases it is not a question of extemporaneous activities or isolated projects, but of a real pedagogical approach included within the education program.

Outdoor Education (OE) is the term generally used to indicate this approach, although there are many different experiences depending on the environment (nature, city, anthropic green areas), type of education (formal or informal), the age group for which they are intended, and the relative peculiarities of methodology (Rickinson et al., 2004). Despite the differences, all these proposals use critical thinking about the learning processes and focus on the educational needs of each new generation. They promote an idea of school not in terms of a specific physical place (traditionally, the classroom), but in terms of active learning experiences in real conditions ('Experiential Education methodology'[1]). In this sense, any place is potentially a school or classroom; especially any outdoor environment, full of stimuli for exploration and discovery activities that improve specific and 'reality' learning, i.e., related to the context in which it develops (Dahlgren, Szczepanski, 1998).

The theoretical and methodological assumptions of the OE are not completely new. They have their roots in the history of pedagogy of different countries, such as the Swiss educator Johann H. Pestalozzi (1746-1827), the German pedagogue Friedrich WA Fröbel (1782-1852), the American educator Margaret McMillan (1860-1931), the English founder of the Scout movement Robert SS Baden-Powell (1857-1941), the Italian Agazzi sisters (Rosa 1866-1951 and Carolina 1870-1945), and many other pedagogists of the international movement for New Education who supported the importance of experiential and cooperative activities (John Dewey, Adolphe Ferrière, Célestin Freinet, Maria Montessori, Giuseppina Pizzigoni...).

These assumptions have not only been made in the domain of pedagogy, but the history of medicine also reminds us that in Europe and the United States during the late nineteenth

---

1 For more information, see Jay Roberts (2012) who examines the theoretical and methodological currents of Outdoor Education.

century an international movement of research and innovation called 'Outdoor schools' was developed. During this movement, doctors, hygienists, political administrators, pedagogues, and educators worked together to deal with the widespread diseases that seriously affected children at that time—tuberculosis, in particular (Châtelet, Lerch, Luc, 2003). A similar tragedy, i.e., the Covid-19 pandemic calls for a similar strategy to tackle issues. Although the outdoor schools of the past were developed within a predominantly medical context (the teaching program alternated with a program of nutrition, treatment and hygienic-sanitary type activities), the experience they teach us today is the idea of encouraging outdoor school activities as a measure albeit indirect against the spread of diseases. Even today, in fact, schools with outdoor curricula represent one of the possible scenarios for rethinking school activities in times of health emergency.[2]

It is important to highlight that progress has been made compared to the past. Over the past twenty-five years, the scientific community has produced a vast amount of international data showing the important benefits of outdoor experiences both for education and instruction and more

2 I point out the National Covid-19 Outdoor Learning Initiative in the Green Schoolyards America web site. 'The National COVID-19 Outdoor Learning Initiative supports schools and districts around the country in their efforts to safely and equitably remain open during the pandemic by using outdoor spaces as strategic, cost-effective solutions to provide access to abundant fresh air.' [https://www.greenschoolyards.org/covid-learn-outside].

generally, for health.[3] Research has shown, in fact, that outdoor activities have a positive effect on every aspect of the person (cognitive, emotional, social, psychological, and physical) and therefore, determine a state of well-being and health[4] for everyone who participates in the activity.

These results have contributed to the development of OE in a more structured way, starting with the definition of the different domains of experience and certainly have favoured its diffusion (even if, as mentioned above, it still remains uneven). There are countries such as Scotland, where the OE approach has found fertile ground in the local culture for many years and outdoor teaching activities are considered among the factors that determine the excellence of schools and educational centres (Beames, Atencio & Ross, 2009). Similarly, in other European and North American countries,

---

3 In the last few years there have been many studies in this field, such as: the guide for outdoor educators in Scotland, edited by Peter Higgins , Chris Loynes and Neville Crowther (1997); the book by Peter H. Jr. Khan (1999) considering the human relationship with nature; the extensive review by Mark Rickinson and colleagues (2004), presenting the data of 150 studies that managed to cover every school level; the report by Geoffrey Godbey (2009), aimed at US health politicians 'when designing recreation and park services and initiatives for the 21st century' (p. 1); the journal 'Journal of Adventure Education and Outdoor Learning' which, since its first publication in 2000, now collects a big repertoire of scientific research; the studies by Ulrika K. Stigsdotter and colleagues (2010), which show how the presence of green areas favours health promotion and stress management among Danish citizens; the very recent research by Nadav L. Sprague and Christine C. Ekenga (2021) on low-income youth of Missouri, which demonstrates the positive impact of nature-based education on the health-related quality of life.

4 The concept of 'health' is here interpreted according to the definition given by the World Health Organisation (WHO) in 1946: 'Health is a state of complete physical, mental and social well-being and not merely the absence of disease or infirmity' [https://www.who.int/about/governance/constitution].

the OE approach has met with the favour of social policies urging governments to carry out actions for the development and implementation of outdoor activities not only for the schools[5], but also for the entire local context (Godbey, 2009).

If, therefore, there are schools and educational services for which OE is an integral part of the local community life, there are some others that, while showing interest in this approach, struggle to find resources and valid motivations for rethinking the traditional educational program. This study intends to respond to this problem by offering a focus on some specific aspects of outdoor school activities. Given the richness of the data produced by international academic research on the benefits of outdoor experiences within instruction and educational courses and the many examples of good practice, this study has considered appropriate to offer a qualitative reading of the topic, to illustrate its meaning and its value in terms of well-being and learning processes.

The questions are:

- In what way does the outdoors favour learning and promote well-being?
- What happens outdoors that doesn't happen inside?

5 Among the growing number of studies on OE within schools, a title to note is the *Handbook of Outdoor Play and Learning* (Waller et al., 2017), published by the members of the European Early Childhood Education Research Association Outdoor Play and Learning SIG (OPAL). This is one of the most exhaustive recent works, as it collects experiences and research from many countries across the world (Europe, North and South America, Australasia, and Asia Pacific countries).

Movement

Movement is the first element I want to highlight as an answer to the question 'What happens outdoors that doesn't happen inside?' Outdoor implies movement; be it action, activity or momentum. It is the natural flow of life, as stated by Aristotle.

Yet, in general at school, movement is often interpreted in negative terms because it is mainly associated with danger, distraction or confusion. It is undeniable, in fact, that students have greater freedom of movement and, consequently, greater possibilities to get away from the eyes of the teacher/educator and run into risky situations outdoors.

The OE approach however, encourages us to discover the positive assessment of movement. In fact, it is possible to consider movement as a 'natural tool' to achieve learning (Neisser, 1976) and develop emotional skills that contribute to establishing positive dynamics of socialisation (Damasio, 2000).

It is important to point out that there are specific conditions in schools for this to occur. It is not enough to go outside to experience meaningful teaching and learning. At school, movement acquires a positive value when it takes place within a setting conceived, designed and organised in an intentional way, so that it is possible on the one hand to promote and support learning experiences and on the other hand to guarantee the health and safety of the participants (House of Commons and Education and Skills Committee, 2005). In these conditions, it is possible to say that the setting directs movement and offers tools to manage it autonomously and appropriately. The children will not move in a random and chaotic way incurring in possible dangerous situations but they will recognise the significance of the experience and they will live the space in a purposeful and attentive way.

I define this kind of movement as 'reflective exploration' referring to John Dewey's concept of 'inquiry',—a movement that arises from an analysis and develops an ordered series of ideas aimed at achieving a specific purpose (Dewey, 1933). Reflective exploration movement is free and at the same time deliberate, pertinent to the experience, functional to the achievement of a specific purpose. Children run, walk, sit, climb, lie down, observe, and explore the outdoors from different points of view and interact with it in different ways. At first glance it might seem like a chaotic situation, but on closer inspection it turns out that every movement has a very specific sense and meaning. Everyone follows their own times, their own rhythms of learning and relationships, finds their own focus of interest, and engages with it in an all-encompassing way, i.e., feeling involved in the 'wholeness' (Chistolini, 2016) of their own person.

This involvement is the most important issue since, in my opinion, because it is what determines the state of well-being and promotes a positive motivation to learn. I think that this involvement is strongly connected with movement because corporeality comes into play, which favours learning processes in which the person is involved not only from a cognitive point of view, but in the wholeness of his or her faculties. As Neisser points out (Neisser, 1976), during any movement all human faculties (emotional, physical, cognitive, psychological...) are united, deeply interwoven with one another; perceiving, feeling and thinking are all part of a whole being. And this is the benefit of movement in terms of well-being—to learn through processes of *embodiment*, that is experienced in the unity and completeness of one's person[6]. Learning can be considered a kind of affirmation of one's person (whole being).

What appears even more interesting is that this 'wholeness' of one's person becomes possible because movement allows one to build a 'relationship with space'. Things learnt through reflective exploration are the result of the dialogue not only with oneself, but also with the surrounding environment and the possibilities it offers. Listen to the rustle of the leaves in the wind and immerse yourself in a state of contemplation. Smell the aroma of the soil at the end of a heavy rainfall and let yourself be carried away in a synaesthetic learning experience. Collaborate with mates to move logs and assemble them creatively. Lie down, run, sit, feel free to choose each one's 'own' posture. Every movement is an emotion, a sensation, a thought which activates memories, considerations and associations of ideas.

Everything is therefore, constantly in movement, including learning. Experiences practised in the context of OE are never an end to themselves, since the exploratory movement is discovery and each discovery has the potential to trigger observation, thought, analysis, debate, research and, finally, new ideas for future projects. In other words,

---

6 On this point, it is very interesting the text by Gregory Bateson, *Steps on an ecology of mind*, in which the relationship between emotions and rationality is investigated. Bateson affirms the impossibility of separating the various faculties that regulate the processes of gaining knowledge into autonomous and independent systems.

learning processes follow a double movement—they develop 'in' movement, i.e., in the very act of moving and therefore, in the relationship between the individual and the environment; but they are also continuously in movement, i.e., they support and sustain an open and dynamic construction of meanings.

Relationship

We can say that OE experiences favour 'learning through relationship' because it is the result of the relationship with oneself, the environment and everything that is part of the experience.

Relationship is the second point I want to focus on, because I think it constitutes a specific attribute of the OE approach that has a positive impact on an individual and in his/her social well-being. In particular, it is concerned with the combination of an individual and the social dimensions. This is because outdoor learning processes tend to be co-constructed and therefore, shared. Research conducted in Italy by Alessandro Bortolotti, Michela Schenetti and Veronica Telese (2020) has shown that OE positively influences interpersonal relationships, encouraging cooperation and mutual help.

We can better understand the meaning and value of this combination of individual and social realms if we consider the role of the environment in offering stimuli that engage everyone in their entirety and uniqueness. For example, how many wonderful things can you discover by simply observing nature with a magnifying glass? Insects, colours, shapes and micro-details previously unknown and that inspire emotions, interests, passions and curiosities. Each discovery represents an opportunity to get in touch with oneself and achieve self-awareness. In this sense, the relationship with the environment favours changes and personal growth, since the maturation of self-awareness activates and strengthens resources, skills and competences.

However, personal growth has an impact on social relations since it inevitably influences the interactions between those who share the experience. The children themselves in fact, often report that while outdoors, they learn new aspects about their classmates and therefore, are able to reconsider their assumptions about them. They are able to establish new dynamics of friendship. For example, children who remain silent in the classroom and tend to express themselves very little or, on the contrary, who exhibit oppositional behaviour and establish conflicting relationships, in OE can change completely and participate actively and collaboratively. They may be enthusiastic and hence, may be able to establish positive interpersonal relationships in which they can take a leadership role. Similarly, children who are among the most studious in the classroom and who always excel, in OE may appear disoriented and with obvious difficulties in interacting since, outdoor learning develops differently than in the classroom. In short, in OE contexts relationships within the group can change completely. Everything can turn upside down and introduce new perspectives. Thus, it is important that the educator and teacher pay attention, in order to stimulate positive motivation for learning in an increasingly efficient way. From this point of view, an interesting factor is verbal interactions. Unlike what happens indoors, it is possible to carry out activities outdoors while conversing with friends. Indeed, in many cases, conversation plays a positive role in building learning processes. Children can discuss the activity they are involved in, exchange ideas and have discussions with each other. In this case, movement supports the rhythm of conversations and helps to offer an instrument of emotional self-regulation (Bortolotti, Schenetti, Telese 2020). For example, in moments of tension or conflict, children have the opportunity to walk, run or move away and isolate themselves. This helps to attenuate emotional overload and re-establish dialogue. In the same way, excessive enthusiasm can be mitigated by satisfying the needs of movement required by one's body (for example, by jumping). In other cases, the conversation may have nothing to do with the activity and becomes an opportunity to gain confidence and tell stories that contribute to create a climate of relaxation which, contrary to what one might imagine, has a strongly positive impact on skills such as attention and concentration.

From inclusion to 'interactions'

When we talk to children about their outdoor experiences, many of them often mention the pleasure of feeling calm, relaxed and free[7]. In particular, they talk about freedom of expression and participation.

These answers demonstrate the human significance of OE contexts in which everyone feels the opportunity to be

7 I refer here to my experience as outdoor educator in Italy, in Early Childhood and Primary schools.

and 'build' themselves. It is worth pausing on this point to develop some reflections on two different but interconnected themes; on one hand, to define what they mean by 'freedom', so that we can understand how it contributes in promoting well-being and learning and on the other hand, to consider the concept of 'inclusion', which is often referred to in these circumstances.

A first meaning of freedom is linked to the temporal dimension. Outdoor learning processes follow 'natural rhythms', that is rhythms set by needs, interests and necessities of the moment. The Italian pedagogist Gianfranco Zavalloni (2005) writes about a 'snail pedagogy', that is pedagogy with slower learning rhythms than those currently adopted in schools and modern society strongly shaped by speed, acceleration and competition[8]. Zavalloni underlines the urgency of recovering more natural learning rhythms, in which everyone can have the opportunity to feel, find and express themselves in a conscious way. From this point of view, OE plays an important role since, learning follows real experiences and not pre-established programs that are little or not at all connected to one's own experience and social reality. Experience Education methodology allows the development of skills and knowledge by learning in a real situation with direct participation. It means that learning follows the questions, curiosities and interests of the children. More precisely, learning follows the 'rhythm' of those questions,

---

8 I would like to stress that Zavalloni considers the Italian education system in particular. However, I believe the same considerations will be relevant to the education system of other countries.

curiosities and interests. To understand how it is possible, here is an example from an experience that I had with children in III grade, primary school. These children were working on a project that they called 'bird's waterland', a water park where the birds can have fun. The idea popped up during a project, where children were invited to rethink creatively on the possible uses of water. They immediately thought of various animals that populate the garden in their school, in particular the large colony of parakeets with which children were used to interaction. The project of the bird's waterland essentially consisted of a fountain. We started working as a group on graphic planning, and we discussed many technical issues, such as materials that could be used, construction times, and the construction processes to be followed. This phase took a long time, the rhythms were 'natural'. There were no pre-fixed times other than those related to the change of teacher, according to the daily timetable. In this sense, rhythms were 'slower' but of higher quality. We had time to make observations, express thoughts and doubts, ask questions and always find new topics to investigate. The children were continuously engaged and they offered many contributions to enrich the project. Many questions were asked about the water supply of the fountain, because in our garden there wasn't a source that could provide water continuously. Working on a solution, we studied the possibility of using renewable energy, and a child proposed the use of solar panels to power the water. Similarly, for the materials to be used in the construction, we decided on an eco-sustainable approach. We chose the bamboo canes collected in the school garden and designed an interlocking construction, without using nails or synthetic glues. Consequently, we addressed many scientific and mathematical issues to design this kind of construction. The most important thing to underline in this experience is that all that was learnt was linked to 'our' project—every single point learned was a result of a need, a necessity or a curiosity. It means that children build 'their' learning in an active way, by following their own rhythms and their natural predispositions. Going back to what Zavalloni says about 'snail pedagogy', in this case slowness was synonymous with 'authentic learning'. This is because children learned on their own by using their creative and critical faculties, in an interdisciplinary way to take actions and finding real solutions to any problems in the physical apparatus of their project. Moreover, in some cases, they went beyond the skills required by national curriculum. Most importantly, 'all' the children were deeply engaged. Natural learning rhythms, precisely because they are natural and not imposed from the outside, allow everyone to find and follow their own learning style, favouring the active participation of everybody.

Multidimensionality of learning styles is the second meaning of the freedom mentioned by children. Learning in an experiential way means participating in a context in which the same subject can be approached in different ways and from different points of view. Similarly, we can say that the same destination can be reached by following different paths. This strategy is used in other teaching methodologies, but in OE contexts it gains an extra amount of significance, i.e., to build autonomously one's own learning 'path'. To understand this extra characteristic, we can consider what happens in early childhood setting. Here, it is common practice to organise the space in different 'stations' (for example: painting, construction, light table, shadow theatre... and so on), where children can explore one topic in different ways. In these cases, in an indoor environment, the educator sets up the stations by choosing 'the paths' and considering which materials and tools are the most appropriate and functional to explore the topic. Outside, instead, children themselves build their own 'path', each one choosing the material and actions that best meet their needs, according to the goal to be achieved. This is especially evident in the case of maths or geometry. Children have a double opportunity—firstly, they can use loose materials (pebbles, sticks, leaves, shells...) to show real calculations and logical processes that would otherwise be difficult to understand as they are abstract concepts; secondly, they can move freely, looking for the material that each one considers most appropriate. Everyone is free to discover their own learning styles and explore them, according to their way of being and feeling. For example, choosing sticks rather than pebbles to make a geometric figure and perform mathematical calculations is not accidental. Each material is different and offers different inputs to learning and getting in touch with oneself. By following another example, it is not accidental that in looking for materials there are some children who explore as wide a space as possible and there are others who only look around where they stand, because movement expresses the rhythm of the mood of the moment. Every movement, every action, talks about itself, affirms its own self.

Affirmation of oneself introduces a further meaning of freedom, that is connected to the dimension of relationships.

Planning an OE experience, in which everyone is free to move and interact with the environment in an educational way, means to arrange a relational setting based on trust. In OE contexts, it is common to see that children, even at a very young age, when left free to explore the environment, clearly demonstrate an innate spirit for exploration. The adult-educator does not leave children to themselves but places himself in a position as neutral as possible (usually behind the children and not in front), to observe and not interfere with the exploratory process. The adult is present not as a leader, but as 'scaffolding' (Vygotskij, 1934), i.e., as a support for the continuous and dynamic construction of meanings.

In OE trust is one of the central key themes and in my opinion, constitutes the element that most influences well-being and positive motivation for learning. Trust means accepting risks, some reasonable and pragmatic risks—falling, getting a little hurt, making a mistake, going back, and starting over again, taking longer than expected, etc. Accepting risks means accepting that everyone and everything has limits. That is to say, accepting people and situations for what they are and not for what we would like them to be—running the risk of facing up to our limits not in order to demonise them but, on the contrary, to know them, be aware of them and develop appropriate strategies for action and learning. From my point of view, therefore, trust means recognizing oneself and others for the uniqueness that they represent. In simpler terms, trust is walking together which is beneficial to one's well-being and engages both children and adults and which, inevitably, stimulates learning.

Walking together helps to focus on the value of the

experience of the moment, perceiving the goal to be achieved not as a demonstration of a performance, but as an input to have fun and feel good together. As mentioned above, OE setting favours positive dynamic interactions, especially cooperation, mutual help, tolerance and dialogue which add a special value to the freedom we are discussing. What is meant here is the value of freedom of participation as 'feeling a part of'—not feeling like a member of this or that other group, but as part of a movement, a change, a real and active action within one's own community. In this sense, OE setting qualify as privileged environments for stimulating experiences in which children can effectively take an action that is not an end in itself, but is always a part of a social dimension. This is the freedom to be oneself in the completeness of one's own person—affirming oneself within the relationship.

These considerations constitute the premise to understanding the topic that I would like to propose for the second theme, that is the concept of 'inclusion'. This term is widely shared in schools at international level and constitutes a priority educational goal. It was introduced recently (about ten years ago, with differences from country to country) to go beyond the term 'integration'. The latter one put the accent on the single, aiming at specific and specialised actions to integrate the individual within the community; the concept of 'inclusion', however, does not indicate single specialised actions, but a continuous daily process that involves the whole group, so everyone can have the opportunity to participate in school life according to his own learning style. A quick search on the web shows many images to represent the meanings of the two terms -integration and inclusion- and, among others, two specifics are usually used. For the concept of integration, we have two circles, one inside the other. The bigger circle is made of dots of one colour, the smaller circle inside the bigger one is made of dots of different colours. For the concept of inclusion, instead, we have a single large circle with dots of one colour in a greater quantity and dots of other colours in lesser quantity. In both cases the circle represents the school community and the coloured dots the children, in particular the different coloured ones represent children with special educational needs.

Based on what has been highlighted so far about the opportunities of OE in terms of well-being and learning, I think that the term 'inclusion' and the image with which it is often represented may confuse their intrinsic meanings. The word 'inclusion' etymologically means 'act of making someone part of an entity', therefore, letting someone into a group to become part of the group. Moreover, in the graph described above, we see that people to be included are represented by a dot with a different colour from the majority. Special attention should be paid in avoiding the mistake of expressing exactly the opposite of what the term communicates: a majority of dots with unique colour that includes—accepts within its own group—a minority of dots with different colours and that, for this reason, it represents an 'otherness'. The paradox, in my opinion, consists of conceiving a homogeneous majority in relation to what could be defined as an 'other'. Claims proposed in this contribution highlight the wholeness of each human being and suggest that well-being and learning develop at their best exactly when we recognize this wholeness. OE contexts focus on exploration, awareness and relationship of trust. It is not expected to have a majority group including someone else. In OE contests we just have individuals who share experiences of know-how and learning. I think it is a mistake to consider children with special educational needs as the 'other' or associate 'otherness' with them, for each one of us represents an otherness.

The problem of the concept of inclusion is philosophical and pedagogical, It refers to the relationship between oneself and the 'other'. Namely, it concerns how one's own subjectivity is built 'in relation' to 'others'. That's why I think it is important to reconsider the meaning of 'inclusion' and look for another term that clearly expresses the different interactions and the social dimension of one's own subjectivity. That is to say, a term that gives an account of the complex and polyphonic dimension, in which learning processes emerge as processes of co-construction.

Personally, I prefer the term 'interactions' because it gives a sense of a relationship of mutual recognition[9], where the practises are based on dialogue, trust, understanding and confrontation. There exists an affirmation of entirety and uniqueness of one's own person, which constitutes a bridge of learning—fundamentally a concrete action 'of' and 'for' peace. The concept of 'interactions' i could simply be represented graphically by the many coloured dots, each one

9 For further reading on the philosophical theme of 'recognition' please see the text by Paul Ricoeur, The Course of Recognition, in which the author argues that through the construct of 'recognition' it is possible to supersede the intimate asymmetry between oneself and the 'other', and construct free relationships that aim to achieve a 'state of peace'.

with a different colour. The circle, then, would have no reason to exist since 'feeling a part of', as specified above, constitutes the freedom to participate in an open real experience, rather than within a specific group.

Considerations

The aim of this proposal was to deepen some specific OE topics to highlight the positive influence they have in promoting well-being and favouring learning activities, especially in terms of personalization of the learning processes. As already mentioned, these positive effects are possible only when the setting of the experience is designed in an intentional and conscious way. This is strictly related to the importance of appropriate professional training, ability to deal with any unexpected events and problems and recognize opportunities. Improvising with children in outdoors spaces is not advised in order to avoid situations of uncontrolled chaos.

One of the reasons for appropriate training and accurate planning concerns the relationship with the natural environment. Not everyone, whether children or adults is at ease relating to the natural environment. This is especially true for those who live in urban areas, where people are usually not familiar with natural environments, and where interaction with nature generally happens within a well-defined space and time, for example a park, weekend family excursion, visit to a farm, outdoor sport (for example trekking or climbing), holidays. The natural and outdoor environment therefore, is not a part of everyday life. Children in many cases love nature but they don't know how to relate and engage with it. Above all and this is my consideration—children don't know that they 'can' have a relationship with nature.

In a city, most of the children and adults are used to being outdoors mainly for recreational or sport activities. This is also the case in schools, where the idea to design outdoor spaces for educational and learning purposes is still in its infancy[10]. In many cases such spaces are set up with equipment for recreational or physical activities (swings, slides, tunnels, climbing ropes, balance beams…), which can be found in many parks of many cities around the world. Children and adults walk by these environments without much awareness, rather than consciously interacting with them. Urban outdoor environments, therefore, appear similar to a container, a vessel not only empty of substance but of a specific meaning that can be easily identified.

The famous French anthropologist Marc Augé (1992) talks about 'non-place', anonymous spaces without an identity and which increasingly dominate modern society: supermarkets, shopping centres, stations, airports. Augé does not explicitly refer to urban natural environments, but perhaps it is not entirely wrong to think of a connection.

The concept of non-place is based on the absence of an 'identity relationship' with the environment, through which it is possible to build a sense of self and of one's own reality. The habit and the ability to have a relationship with the environment (any environment, natural or anthropic as it is) are being lost. In particular, for those who live in cities, nature is an environment that is increasingly becoming a 'place-

10 Here I refer primarily to the situation in Italian schools.

other' and people are losing familiarity interacting with it. In this sense, the risk is that nature will become an empty and anonymous space, a non-place. More and more urban children experience significant emotional distress, among other things, due to fear of animals (especially insects) or to a hypersensitivity to touch that causes disgust and a sense of dirtiness. Above all, the most important point is that the older we get the more we devalue the environment, and we lose our spontaneous relationship with nature through which it is possible to know, become aware of and rethink oneself and one's life (for example, writing a poem inspired by a specific natural element, elaborating a composition using natural elements or observing the growth of leaves in a plant to derive mathematical laws).

It is therefore important to keep in mind these critical aspects, because only professional training and accurate planning of settings would be helpful in managing the experience in an appropriate way. What in my opinion represents the greatest opportunity for the OE, in terms of well-being and learning, is to live such experiences as precious moments to re-appropriate places of identity and allow the development of more active and conscious people and citizens.

REFERENCES

Auge, M. *Non-Places: Introduction to an Anthropology of Supermodernity*. Translated by John Howe. Verso Books, 1995.

Beames, S., M. Atencio and H. Ross. "Taking Excellence Outdoors." *Scottish Educational Review* 41, no. 2 (2009): 32–45.

Bortolotti, A., M. Schenetti and V. Telese. "L'Outdoor Education come possible approccio inclusivo. Una ricerca nei servizi educativi zero-sei del Comune di Bologna." *Italian Journal of Special Education for Inclusion* 1 (2020): 417–433.

Chatelet, A. M., D. Lurch and J. N. Luc. "L'école de plein air: Une expérience pédagogique et architecturale dans l'Europe du XX siècle, Open-Air Schools: An Educational and Architectural Venture in Twentieth-Century Europe." *Revue francaise de pedagogie* 147 (2004): 133–134.

Chistolini, S. *Pedagogia della natura. Pensiero e azione nell'educazione della scuola contemporanea: Asilo nel bosco, Jardin-Escola João de Deus, Outdoor Education*. Franco Angeli, 2016.

Dahlgren, L. and A. Szczepanski. "Outdoor Education: Literary education and sensory experience." *University of Sweden* (1998).

Damasio, A.R. *Emozione e coscienza*. Adelphi, 2000.

Godbey, Geoffrey. "Outdoor Recreation, Health, and Wellness: Understanding and Enhancing the Relationship." *RFF Discussion Paper*, no. 9–21 (2009). http://dx.doi.org/10.2139/ssrn.1408694

Hartig, T., M. Richard, S. De Vries and H. Frumkin. "Nature and Health." *Annual Review of Public Health* 35 (2014): 207–228.

Higgins, P., C. Loynes and N. Crowther. *A guide for outdoors in Scotland*. Adventure Education, 1997.

United Kingdom, Parliament, Parliamentary Business. *House of Commons - Education and Skills,* Second Report. UK, 2005. House of Commons - Education and Skills - Second Report (parliament.uk)

Neisser, U. *Cognition and Reality: Principles and Implications of Cognitive Psychology*. W H Freeman & Co., 1976.

Rickinson, M., et al. *A Review of research on outdoor learning*. Shrewsbury: National Foundation For Educational Research and King's College, 2004. https://www.informalscience.org/sites/default/files/Review%20of%20research%20on%20outdoor%20learning.pdf

Ricoeur, P. *The Course of Recognition*. Harvard University Press, 2007.

Roberts, J.W. *Beyond learning by doing: Theoretical Currents in Experiential Education*. Routledge, 2012.

Sprague, N. L. and C. C. Ekenga. "The impact of nature-based education on health-related quality of life among low income youth: Results from an intervention study." *Journal of Public*

Health (2021) 1–8. https://doi.org/10.1093/pubmed/fdaa243

Stigsdotter, U. K., O. Ekholm, J. Schipperijn, M. Toftager, F. Kamper-Jorgensen, and T. B. Randrup. "Health promoting outdoor environments: associations between green space, and health, health-related quality of life and stress based on a Danish national representative survey." *Scand J Public Health* 38, no. 4 (2010): 411–7.

Vygotskij, L.S. *Thought and Language*. MIT Press, 1934.

Waller, Tim, Eva Arlemalm-Hagser, Ellen B. H. Sandseter, Libby Lee-Hammond, Kristi Lekies and Shirley Wyve, eds. *The SAGE handbook of outdoor play and learning*. SAGE, 2017.

Zavalloni, Gianfranco. *La pedagogia della lumaca. Per una scuola lenta e non violenta*. EMI, 2015.

KARI SUTTON

Educator, speaker, and author from Australia

Kari has helped over 25,000 children, parents, and educators with evidence-based strategies, tools and approaches to foster children's positive mental health. During her 25-year career in education, Kari has held a front-row seat in dealing with the escalating crisis in children's mental health. She deconstructs the research and provides practical, easy-to-use tools and strategies that plant the seeds of resilience and emotional well-being in our children. She launched her second book 'Raising a Mentally Fit Generation' in 2020.

FOUR

HELPING CHILDREN MANAGE THEIR EMOTIONS

Children with higher levels of emotional intelligence enjoy increased self-confidence, better performance in school, better physical health and healthier social relationships.

John Gottman (1997, p.18)

WE ALL experience anger, fear, frustration, sadness, rejection, disappointment, jealousy, and guilt at different times—they are simply part of being 'human'. Emotionally healthy people can label their emotions and manage their emotional reactions to external events and strong feelings without yelling, throwing things or damaging property. They can express a broad range of emotions and don't get stuck in a particular emotion for a long while. While they might feel angry, frustrated, sad, anxious, or scared, these feelings don't prevent them from managing any situation well since they have developed emotional agility.

Everything in this chapter has been drawn from research related to emotional and psychological wellbeing. It takes key findings from the new field of Positive Psychology and combines them with valuable knowledge from

Developmental Cognitive Neuroscience and emotional intelligence, to provide evidence-based strategies and ideas about how parents can help their children develop emotional intelligence in order to thrive. As a researcher and educator, I have made it my goal to follow the emerging research and translate it into simple, practical strategies and tools, which with can immediately implemented in the day-to-day lives of parents I work with, to sow seeds of emotional wellbeing in their children and help them develop habits that will last a lifetime.

Children's ability to understand and manage emotions develops over time. When they are young, they need help with understanding emotions. The first thing they need to learn is to recognise and name emotions, as this lays the foundation for acknowledging and managing their feelings and emotions, as they grow older. As children mature, they'll learn more strategies to manage their emotions without anybody's help. Understanding and managing emotions is also called 'emotional regulation' which is an important part of self-regulation.

I always encouraged children and young people I worked with to identify and express what they think and feel, and to be considerate towards the thoughts and feelings of others. The results were often extraordinary. Kids as young as seven were very self-aware, making statements such as:

- I don't like it and get angry when my friends don't want to play with me. I yell at them to try and get them to understand, but it only makes things worse.
- I feel incredibly anxious in school because I'm worried that I am going to be slower than my friends at the

work, and they might make fun of me.

- I get angry when Mum and Dad work all the time and can't help me with my school stuff or take me to soccer. It makes me want to throw things, but I don't because then they'd get mad.

After working with thousands of families, I came to realise that as adults, we frequently underestimate our child's ability to process and understand complex emotions. We assume that they're less capable of processing emotions and hence, we try to protect them from unpleasant, thornier subjects. We usually avoid to bring up such topics, let alone discuss them. But we must realize that if we create safe environments where children can openly talk about their feelings and trust that they will be listened to and not judged, they will be able to navigate through their emotions in a more positive way, and will also find it easier to express and talk about them. Hence, as they begin talking, we should teach our children to identify and talk about their feelings. They can comprehend and lead mature conversations about their emotions if we explicitly teach them the skills and language needed.

Research from the Yale Centre for Emotional Intelligence (2019) has shown that emotional intelligence, sometimes shortened to EQ, predicts over 54% of the variation in success in people's relationships, quality of life, long-term health and effectiveness at work and school. This is reflected in the fact that children and young people with high EQ stay in school longer, receive better grades, make healthier choices than their peers who have lower levels of EQ, and are less likely to end up in jail. By teaching our kids how to recognise their feelings, understand where they come from and how to deal with them, we are providing them with some of the most crucial skills to be happy and achieve success throughout their lives.

One of the most important gifts we can give our children is the ability to connect with others and sustain these friendships. Friendship and social skills in early childhood are more predictive of outcomes in adulthood than academic skills with a significant correlation between children's social skills in kindergarten and their wellbeing at age of twenty-five. Children who displayed social competence were more likely to finish high school, go to college, find a job, and stay out of the justice system than those who exhibited lower levels of social competence. Just like any relationship, friendships take efforts, and we must provide our children with the tools, strategies and skills they need, to be a good friend and make and keep good friends in life. One of the most critical skills they can develop in order to be a good friend and make and keep good friends is understanding and managing their emotions.

In another study, researchers from Penn State and Duke University (2015) interviewed kindergarten teachers about children's social and emotional skills—how well they shared, listened to others, resolved problems with their friends and were helpful. If we want to raise kind, empathic and generous kids it is critical that we focus on their emotional literacy and development.

The researchers followed these children until they were young adults to investigate what happened to them. They discovered that the children with the highest social and emotional competency scores in kindergarten functioned better overall. They were twice as likely to obtain a university degree and more likely to have full-time jobs by the age of twenty-five. The children who had trouble cooperating, listening and resolving conflict were more likely to drop out of high school, have legal problems and substance abuse issues. For every one-point decline in social competencies at age five, a child had a 67% higher possibility of being arrested in early adulthood, a 52% higher possibility of binge drinking, and an 82% higher probability of living in public housing (or at least being on the waitlist). These results were independent of ethnicity, being born to teenage parents, poverty or family stressors.

As children grow, they learn different social and emotional skills at different rates – there is no one linear model to summarize how emotional intelligence should look like in children of different ages. Please don't panic if your child is already older than five – the good news is the skills of emotional intelligence can be taught, and children can learn them at any age. Daniel Goleman (1995) has identified five components of emotional intelligence which are self-awareness, self-regulation, empathy, social skills and motivation.

Self-awareness is the ability to identify and understand your own emotions. To become self-aware, it's essential that children can observe, recognise and name their emotions, notice different emotional reactions they have, and understand the relationship between the emotions they feel and the ways they behave. They also need to develop an understanding of what impact their own actions, moods and emotions have on others.

Self-regulation enables us to regulate and manage how

we react to our emotions. This does not mean that we expect children to hide their true feelings or not express their emotions. We need to help them understand that there is a right time, place and appropriate way to express their emotions and impulses so they can stay in control and not physically or verbally lash out at others.

Empathy is our ability to understand how others feel. It requires us to recognise other people's emotions and then respond to them in appropriate ways based on this information. For example, when your child recognises that their friend is sad, having empathy guides their response to them, if they try to cheer them up or help them feel better.

Social skills support our children's ability to interact well with others and manage their social relationships.

When children understand their own emotions, as well as the feelings of others, they can apply this information when they communicate and interact with other people. This helps them build and manage relationships and connections with people they encounter every day.

The motivation that Goleman refers to is intrinsic motivation, where children have a sense of what's important in life. They aren't constantly driven by external rewards. They instead do what makes them happy, for instance being kind to others.

One of the ways parents can help kids develop self-awareness, self-regulation, empathy, social skills and intrinsic motivation is through Professor John Gottman's Emotion Coaching approach. Professor Gottman developed this approach after analysing the parenting of hundreds of couples with children aged four or five. He gave them questionnaires, conducted thousands of hours of interviews, observed their behaviour in his lab, videotaped sessions of the children playing with their best friends, monitored their heart rates, respiration, blood flow and sweating as well as taking urine samples from the children to measure stress-related hormones. He continued to follow the development and progress of these children through adolescence, conducting more interviews and observations. The children with parents who used emotion coaching techniques were able to calm themselves faster (their heart rates slowed much more quickly than their peers), they related to their friends better, had more focused attention, and could manage tough social situations in later childhood if they were getting bullied or teased.

There are five crucial steps to emotion coaching:

1. Being aware of children's emotions

As parents, we should be aware of both our own and our children's emotions. We should be able to recognise what we feel and be sensitive to what emotions others—especially our children experience. Feelings frequently precede outbursts. Thus, we should be able to understand and acknowledge the struggles of our children and help them manage their feelings, before they lose control. This step is very similar to Goleman's first component of EQ where we help our children understand that emotions are a natural and valuable part of life that provides them with the information they can use to make appropriate decisions. Watch your children, listen to their language, note changes in their facial expressions, body language or the tone of their voice. You will be able to learn how they express different emotions, both physically and verbally. This way, you can help your child respond to their big feelings in healthy ways and provide guidance before their emotions escalate into challenging behaviours.

Parents must be afraid of showing emotions in front of their kids as long as it's done in a respectful and constructive way. When we model how to handle difficult and uncomfortable feelings effectively, our children will be better prepared for life. If we hide our emotions, our kids are less capable of handling negative, unpleasant emotions in healthy ways.

2. Viewing emotions as an opportunity for connection and teaching

Even though it seems counterintuitive, it is best to connect with your child, when they might experience negative emotions, and throw tantrums. Parents may use it as a moment significant to teaching and learning. I admit this doesn't feel like the most rational thing to do when your child is hurling objects or verbal abuse at you, and stopping misbehaviour is the priority. But we should handle this in a specific way, so the child knows it's about their behaviour and not them personally. When our children encounter challenging situations like not wanting to share a toy, falling out with a friend, a bad grade on a test, being teased or not being selected for a sporting team, it is a wonderful opportunity to connect with them, demonstrate empathy for how they are feeling and teach them ways to handle those difficult feelings. This way, we can demonstrate to our children that we care about them and that we are on their side, an ally who will help them figure out how to solve their problem.

When we're upset about something, we do not appreciate people invalidating our feelings by asking us to get over the matter. Children don't like it either. We feel any emotions for a reason, and we need to give our kids the time and space to feel their feelings, without trying to change them. To acknowledge our own emotions and validate our feelings is crucial to navigate through them. The next time your child feels upset because something has gone wrong in a game or at the playground, tell them, 'It's okay to feel disappointed. I'll sit here with you so you can feel it until it passes.'

3. Listening empathetically and validating feelings

When we listen empathetically to our children's concerns, we are showing them that we respect them, take their emotions seriously, and understand how they feel. We need to avoid judging or criticising our children's emotions or saying things like, 'You shouldn't feel that way' or 'Everything is going to be fine' as these are dismissive statements. They don't work with adults in a moment of crisis, and they certainly won't work with our children. Instead, we need to validate their feelings and show them that we understand and are on their side. We don't have to accept or validate their behaviour if it's inappropriate, but we do need to demonstrate our care and empathy for them. You can do this by saying something simple like, 'I noticed you were frowning when I mentioned going swimming at school today' and then wait for their response. Once they start opening up, we can help them find ways to understand, label and cope with their uncomfortable feelings. Remember, you are validating the feeling, not the behaviour. You can validate that your child is sad, angry, or scared without validating that they hit their sibling. Try saying, 'I can see how angry you are right now'.

4. Helping the child verbally label emotions

If children label their emotions and talk about feelings that scare them, they will be more apt at dealing with them, and the scary feelings will dissipate more quickly. As adults, we have words to describe our feelings; our children don't. We need to help them develop a broad emotional vocabulary so they can label the feelings they experience. Dan Siegel in his book *The Whole-Brain Child* (2011) proves that describing and labelling our intense feelings calm our nervous system and help us to recover from upsetting situations or incidents more quickly. Putting their feelings into words helps children express their experiences and eventually, transform their big, scary, overwhelming feelings into something regular ones which can be managed (with some guidance and help at first).

5. Setting limits while helping the child problem-solve

Once we have acknowledged the emotion that sits behind the tantrum or other challenging inappropriate behaviour and have helped our children label it, we then need to ensure that our children understand that some behaviours are inappropriate and must not be tolerated.

All feelings are acceptable—but every behaviour is not.

Every emotion is valid, though we need to make it very clear that angry feelings are okay but violent, destructive and aggressive behaviour is not. We need to let children know that it is ok to feel any emotion, they can get really angry, or be very scared, but we also need to make it clear that they can choose how they respond to these big emotions. Your child has every right to be angry at someone, but that does not give them the right to hit them. They can be very disappointed that the ice cream shop is out of their favourite flavour, but that doesn't mean it is appropriate to roll around on the floor, yelling and screaming.

Always keep in mind that emotions are frequently what drives children's behaviour. When they are experiencing intense emotions, children and teenagers aren't going to stop in the middle of everything and say, 'Could you please be patient with me I'm struggling with my feelings and haven't got a better way of expressing them right now,' and may be acting it out—their behaviour is showing us they're not coping and need our support.

We must set limits and boundaries to ensure that our children know what is socially acceptable. You need to be firm and guide your child into considering more appropriate ways to manage their negative feelings. For example, you might say something like, 'You're mad at Jenny because she took that doll from you. I would be upset and angry too. But it's not okay for you to pull her hair. What could you do instead?' We need to model appropriate ways to deal with big emotions and teach them specific strategies and tools they can use. You have listened empathetically, helped her label her feelings, and set limits on her misbehaviour—now it's time to help her develop problem-solving skills, as you won't always be there to solve the problem. We need to provide scaffolding and guidance for our kids to come up with ideas about possible solutions that are effective and consider other people's feelings.

When you observe your child processing something emotional, which is frequently a slower process for kids, acknowledge what you're observing and praise their efforts. If you notice them taking deep breaths and doing the activity that scares them—when they might once have avoided it or run away, or if they went outside and had a jump on the trampoline instead of hitting their sibling who'd wrecked their Lego creation—acknowledge their behaviour accordingly and praise their efforts. This provides them with positive feedback, and a dopamine hit that ignites the brain, for making a healthy choice.

Please don't put unrealistic expectations on yourself about following these five steps all the time—it's not always possible to do this in the heat of the moment, but one must strive. Dr Gottman discovered that even if parents only do all five steps 20–25 % of the time, this still provides children with a strong foundation of EQ skills that will benefit them for the rest of their life.

Children need to experience the kaleidoscope of human emotions in order to develop emotional wellbeing and resilience. If they don't experience what it's like to be disappointed or sad, they are unlikely to develop the skills to manage those feelings or the ability to empathise with others. However, due to our innate negative biases, the negative emotions which serve to alert us to potential threats and dangers far outnumber the positive emotions we experience. This is especially true in childhood, when our emotional awareness is amplified for possible threats. This can trigger children's protective emotions to become overactive, which flood their bodies with the stress hormones adrenaline and cortisol and can leave their stress response permanently switched on. When this happens, there is a greater chance of them developing anxiety disorders and other emotional problems.

Professor Barbara Fredrickson (2009) and her colleagues at the University of Carolina found that positive emotions undo the effects of stress and turn off the stress response by replacing the stress hormones with serotonin and dopamine. This calms us physically and fuels our prefrontal cortex (the thinking part of our brain), enabling us to think more clearly and make effective, rational decisions. Fredrickson (2009) asserts that positive emotions are vital to our emotional wellbeing and mental health.

When children experience positive emotions such as love, gratitude, optimism, hope, contentment, kindness, enthusiasm and confidence, it has a powerful impact on their wellbeing and fosters an inner calm and positivity. It's therefore critically important that we help children experience and build positive emotions on a daily basis so that they learn how to generate their own positivity and create a positive balance of emotions that builds lasting resilience and wellbeing.

Finding effective ways to help your child cope with big emotions has never been more important. Here are some suggestions for activities that you can use to help your children develop self-awareness, self-regulation, empathy, and social skills.

1. Share your feelings

All of us experience a wide range of emotions—frustration, disappointment, anger, fear, sadness, jealousy, happiness, and it's a good idea to share these with your children whenever it's appropriate to do so. We don't want to burden our kids with our emotions and experiences, but we should be able to make them understand that, even we feel those things at different times and have had to learn how to manage them.

2. Feelings binoculars

This activity develops children's awareness about emotions, what they feel like in their bodies and can help them identify emotions they are feeling. You will need two cardboard rolls, some glue to stick them together, some pens to decorate them with and possibly some string if you'd like your children to hang them around their neck. Talk to your child about how binoculars work and describe how they make things to appear closer. You may next explain that you are going to make a pair of binoculars that allows them to look inside their bodies and see how they feel.

Once the binoculars are finished, model how to use them by using them on yourself. Look at your feet first and next move up your body to explain what you notice in your body and name how you feel. Your child can now explore their findings with the binoculars. If they display any trouble identifying what happens in their bodies, talk about other examples when you have used your binoculars to notice when your tummy was feeling upset and your heart was pounding because you were nervous about an important meeting.

3. Emotion squeeze balls

These balls help children identify the facial expressions that represent different feelings. You'll need yellow balloons, permanent markers, rice and a funnel.

To draw the facial expressions of different emotions on the balloons, you'll need to blow them up a little bit and hold the end so that the air doesn't come out. Then talk with your child about what facial expressions match different emotions and see if they can guess the one you're drawing on the balloon. Once you've drawn the face, let it dry for several minutes and then put the funnel in the open neck of the balloon. Pour the rice into the balloon to fill it, leaving the neck section free so you can tie a knot.

Keep them in a container your child can access and they can select which emotion they feel at the time based on the facial expression – they can also be used as stress balls and fidget toys.

4. Energy thermometer

This activity will help your child notice how much energy they have inside, what they are feeling and how they can manage their energy. Draw a picture of a temperature gauge or thermometer, with a picture of a fish at the bottom and a volcano at the top. Then ask your child if they feel calm like the fish swimming in the water or are in a turbulent state like the volcano. Talk about how different feelings can make their body have different levels of energy, and brainstorm ways through which they can be more calm. This could be doing things like going outside and running around, deep belly breathing, colouring in or listening to music.

5. Identify healthy coping strategies

Your child should know that it is possible for people to lose control. However, we need to help them identify different coping strategies they can utilise when they need to regain control. It's important to make sure that you identify appropriate coping strategies for your child as each child is different and will need different methods to help them calm down. Some coping strategies that might be useful are: listening to music, colouring-in or drawing, going to a quiet space for leisure, squeezing a stress ball, jumping on a trampoline, blowing bubbles, drinking a glass of cold water, punching a pillow, kicking a ball outside, going for a run-around, scribbling on a piece of paper or ripping paper up. Once you have identified them together, you can talk about how they can use them when they need them both at home and school.

You can also make some visual reminders of strategies and ideas for coping by placing photos of the activities on small, laminated cards and having them stuck on the fridge or threaded on to a keyring they could carry in their pocket. In this way healthy coping strategies will be readily available, when their emotions escalate.

Children learn by watching their parents and other significant adults in their lives and are quick to pick up and mimic behaviours—either positive or negative—that they have seen being exhibited. It's vital, therefore, that we are good role models and practise what we preach. When we are upset, we must acknowledge our emotions, and use our coping strategies to regain control and work through the situation.

6. Make a coping skills plan

A key part of successful coping is being prepared. Work with your children when they are calm to develop a coping skills plan for when they are feeling big emotions. Help them identify which coping skills work best for them. Their plan should include:

- Warning signs indicating any elevation in their emotional faculty
- A list of 3-5 coping skills that they will use when they notice the warning signs
- Steps for how to seek help from adults

7. Create a coping kit

When your children plan anything, you should encourage them to gather the supplies and equipment which they'll need to engage in the chosen coping skills (even as adults we have strategies and tools that help us remain calm). For example, they might like to look at photos of the beach or puppies, they might want to eat a certain type of food, solve a puzzle or use some putty. Together you can collect those resources and put them in a specified, easily accessible place that they can access when in need. This will then become their coping kit.

8. Practice Coping Skills

It can be difficult for children to use a new skill for the first time especially when emotions are running high. So, it's best if your children can practice their new coping skills before trying them out in the heat of the moment.

9. Watch movies together

Most children love movies, take the time to watch movies together that can help them learn about emotions. The following movies are some good examples: *Inside Out, Brave, Zootopia, Frozen, Finding Nemo, Charlotte's Web, Harry Potter, Coco, Encanto, Big Hero 6, Paddington, Monsters Inc, The Lorax.*

10. Read books about emotions

Books play a critical role in children's lives. Picture books are an ideal way to introduce concepts to children. They can help children learn how to empathise with others by empathising with the characters they read about. Kids can observe characters in books going through hard times and overcoming them and possibly see themselves reflected in those stories. Books can provide a vocabulary for kids struggling to articulate how they feel and can let them know that other people feel that way too sometimes. Reading together builds connection and closeness between a parent and a child, provides a shared vocabulary for family life and makes memories that children will cherish for a lifetime. Reading does not have to be an expensive activity—many families I work with plan weekly trips to the library where they have fun selecting books together. The following books provide a good starting point to explore emotions and how they can be managed.

Understanding feelings

The way I feel by Janan Cain
The grouchy ladybug by Eric Carle

Alexander and the terrible, horrible, no good, very bad day by Judith Viorst
The feelings book by Todd Parr
All kinds of feelings by Sheri Safran
My many coloured days by Dr Seuss
In my heart: A book of feelings by Jo Witek
The colour monster by Anna Llenas
A book of feelings by Amanda McCardie
The great big book of feelings by Mary Hoffman
Today I feel silly and other moods that make my day by Jamie Lee Curtis
Grumpy monkey by Suzanne Lang
What to do when you're feeling blue by Andi Cann
Visiting feelings by Lauren Rubenstein

Feeling scared

The fun book of scary stuff by Emily Jenkins
Scaredy squirrel by Emily Watt
Nana in the city by Lauren Castillo
Courage by Bernard Waber
Max the brave by Ed Vere
When I'm feeling scared by Trace Moroney
The I'm not scared book by Todd Parr
Brave as can be: A book of courage by Jo Witek

Managing anger and other big feelings

When Sophie Gets Angry—Really, Really Angry by Molly Bang
When I'm Feeling Angry by Trace Moroney
When I Feel Angry by Cornelia Maude Spelman
When Miles Got Mad by Sam Kurtzman-Counter

Mad Isn't Bad by Mundy Micahelene
How to Take the GRRR Out of Anger by Elizabeth Verdick
Don't Rant and Rave on Wednesday by Adolph Moser
What To Do When Your Temper Flares by Dawn Huebner
Zach Gets Frustrated by William Mulcahy
Crankenstein by Samantha Berger
Wemberley Worried by Kevin Henkes
Beautiful Oops by Barney Saltzberg
You Are Your Strong by Danielle Dufayet
Crabbypants by Julie Gassman

In a nutshell

- All emotions serve a useful purpose in our lives; be it both the positive and negative emotions. Our emotions are simply data telling us things about what we experience. They are signs that something might be right or wrong, and help us to communicate it with others around us.
- The primary pathways in the brain that enable us to recognise, understand and manage our emotions are formed in early childhood. These are substantially impacted by parent-child interactions and children's observations of the ways their parents manage their emotions and regulate their behaviour. As parents, we need to nurture our children's positive emotions on a daily basis so that we can help them create a positive balance of emotions in their lives.
- We need to explicitly teach our kids the skills of emotional intelligence—how to recognise their

feelings, understand where they come from, and how to deal with them. This will help them regulate their behaviour, develop emotional agility and navigate social complexities.

REFERENCES

Fredrickson, B. L. *Positivity*. New York: Three Rivers Press, 2009.

Goleman, D. *Emotional Intelligence: Why It can matter more than IQ*. Bantam Books, 1995.

Gottman, J. and J. DeClaire. *Raising an Emotionally Intelligent Child*. Simon & Schuster, 1997.

Jones, D. E., M. Greenberg and M. Crowley. "Early Social-Emotional Functioning and Public Health: The Relationship between Kindergarten Social Competence and Future Wellness." *American Journal of Public Health* 105, no. 11 (2015): 2283–2290. https://doi.org/10.2105%2FAJPH.2015.302630

Siegel, Daniel J. and T. Bryson. *The Whole-Brain Child: Revolutionary Strategies to Nurture Your Child's Developing Mind*. New York: Delacorte Press, 2011.

Yale School of Medicine, "Yale Center for Emotional Intelligence." https://medicine.Yale.edu/childstudy/services/community-and-schools-programs/center-for-emotional-intelligence/

DR VASAVVI ACHARJYA

Early Childhood Education Expert, Edupreneur, Social Activist, Mentor, Child Rights Enthusiast, Author, Ex-trainer at TISS.

Dr Vasavvi is the Founder and Managing Director of Inner I Foundation Pvt Ltd (IIFPL). In 2013, she launched Tender Petals Preschools, which was featured in the Forbes India GPTS issue of Great Indian Preschools 2019. She moved into social work and founded D N Acharya Foundation for Children and Women Welfare in 2014 and its global initiative the Early Childhood Development Forum in 2019.

GIRIJA GOPINATH

Girija's passions are understanding the elements that make us human, especially our commonalities and our uniqueness. An MBA with a specialisation in Human Resources and over 20 years of experience in varied industries like Advertising, FMCG, Express, Health-care.

FIVE

THE IMPACT OF MINDFULNESS

HAVE YOU gotten into a shower, just to suddenly find yourself all dressed-up for work? Ever realised you have driven yourself home but haven't really been paying attention to the journey? Did you begin to read a book and find yourself at the end of it without knowing how you reached there?

We all have, at various points experienced these in our day-to-day life. These are some of the examples of mindlessness.

So, then what is Mindfulness? To understand the concept of Mindfulness it is important for us to know what exactly mindlessness is.

Mindlessness is a state of mind, we often refer to as 'autopilot'. Brain scans have revealed that when our mind wanders, it switches into 'autopilot' mode, enabling us to continue our tasks without any conscious thought.

The autopilot mode seems to be run by a set of brain structures called the Default Mode Network (DMN).

It was discovered in the 1990s, when researchers noticed that people lying in brain scanners show patterns of brain activity even when they aren't really doing anything.

This research provided the first evidence that our brains are active even when we aren't consciously putting our minds to work. But what does the DMN do? Several studies have found that it seems to be involved in assessing past events and planning the future. This is also known as Mind-Wandering.

To investigate, researchers asked twenty-eight volunteers to learn a card game while lying in an fMRI brain scanner. At the game, each person was presented with four cards. They were then given a fifth and were asked to match it to one of the four cards. But the participants were not made aware of the rules—they didn't know whether to match the cards by colour or shape, for example. Through much trial and error, each person figured it out after a few rounds.

While this happened, their brain activity resembled patterns that are typical of learning minds. But as the game continued, and the participants knew how to match the cards without much thinking, their brain activity resembled those of using the DMN and their responses became faster and more accurate.

This suggests that when we 'switch off,' our brains go into an autopilot mode that allows us to perform tasks reasonably without thinking much about them. This might also help explain why some tasks, such as playing a well-known tune on a musical instrument suddenly seem much more difficult when you go from doing them absent-mindedly to consciously thinking about them.

A brief History on Mindfulness

Mindfulness has been a part of human lives since time immemorial and is said to have its origins in eastern and Buddhist philosophy. Mindfulness has been intertwined with Hinduism for millennia. From *Bhagavad Gita*'s discussions of yoga to Vedic meditation, the history of Hinduism reads in part like a history of mindfulness. But it is imperative to consider arguments contesting the reduction of the history of mindfulness to Buddhism and Hinduism, as mindfulness also has roots in the beliefs of Judaism, Christianity and Islam (Trousselard et al., 2014).

The concept of mindfulness was introduced to the western world by Jon Kabat-Zinn who secularised the principles of mindfulness by untangling them from the religious and cultural strings attached to them. He metamorphosed mindfulness into formalised mindfulness-based intervention which was widely accepted for its benefits in stress reduction. In 1979 he started a stress-reduction centre at the University of Massachusetts Medical School, developing an eight-week Mindfulness-Based Stress Reduction (MBSR) course. Non-religious mindfulness meditation was widely accepted for its numerous benefits.

In the Indian context, mindfulness practices have been a part of our daily lives, in the form of awakening one's senses to the 'here and now' rather than going back and forth to the past and future. We often see our ancient texts mention the teachings of revered gurus who taught their disciples (students) to hunt blindfolded, to shoot in the dark and hit the bird's eye, to chew every morsel in the mouth and experience the flavour and so forth. These were simple mindfulness activities that held within them the power to control one's mind and tune in to the present and stay in the moment.

Mindfulness and the Science of It

The human brain is a complex network comprising of hundreds of trillions of synapses that help the brain cells to communicate internally. There are over 80–100 billion neurons that form these connections and even with advanced scientific research, it is difficult to understand the complete functioning of the human brain. Mindfulness and meditation are said to have a positive impact on the neural network and has been a popular topic for research and experiment.

There have been many studies associated with mindfulness, the most popular being Mindfulness-Based Stress Reduction (MBSR) and Mindfulness-Based Cognitive Therapy (MBCT). This research is done by eminent scientists whose goal was to figure out how the adoption of mindfulness offers several benefits to the users.

1. Mindfulness-Based Stress Reduction (MBSR)

The MBSR technique was pioneered by Dr Jon Kabat-Zinn who conducted a study of chronically ill patients, grouped together, who weren't responding well to traditional treatments. An eight-week stress-reduction program, now termed as MBSR improved the mental and physical health of the patients considerably and they started responding to their treatment in a positively.

MBSR is a group-based approach where people are primarily assisted with dealing with stress and anxiety-related mental health issues. The study involved the group to combine meditation, yoga, and other techniques to alleviate the stress. MBSR is one of the leading techniques that is used by the most mindfulness training program for everyone including corporate, entrepreneurs, children, and patients.

2. Mindfulness-Based Cognitive Therapy (MBCT)

MBCT is another popular group program developed by Segal, Teasdale, and Williams. The key idea that forms the foundation of the MBCT program is to help people get rid of unproductive and negative thoughts. It also helps with aligning their behavioural thoughts and emotional responses to the situation and environment. The study employs psychological techniques to resolve mental and mood disorders that otherwise affect their functionality.

Cognitive Behavioural Therapy (CBT) used for MBCT uses mindful breathing along with meditation to help patients suffering from chronic depression and anxiety. The training is especially for chronic patients who relapse occasionally and require conditioning to deal with their mental condition.

Mindfulness Basics and Definitions

> 'Mindfulness means paying attention in a particular way—on purpose, in the present moment, and non-judgmentally.'
>
> –Jon Kabat-Zinn

There are many definitions of mindfulness, and all ask us to meet each moment of our lives with clarity, curiosity and openness. For, clarity is seeing what is right here, right now—the way it is, rather than what we expected, wanted or feared would be here. Curiosity on the other hand, is approaching our life with an attitude of wonder—'What is this?' rather than 'Oh no, I hate this!' Being curious helps to avoid run in fear or being lost in fantasies. It also feels good. It is like an internal reward. Openness is about meeting our experience without judgment. Practising openness is very difficult because we go against the grain. In fact, we are conditioned to submit to the automated negative thoughts and to immediately judge our experiences in binaries.

Mindfulness Simplified

These days, the word 'mindfulness' is everywhere and practicing it is helpful. Let us try to understand mindfulness is.

Mindfulness is different to different people. For some, mindfulness is the practice of acknowledging what they feel without judging their emotions or sensations as they experience them. It is the art of being in the moment. To be mindful is to be fully aware of how we experience the present. By maintaining a moment-by-moment awareness of our thoughts, feelings, bodily sensations, and surrounding environment, through a gentle and nurturing lens we accommodate the practice of Mindfulness in our day-to-day life.

It is also a shift in the way that we pay attention. And through that subtle shift our entire world can transform from the inside out. When it comes to Mindfulness there is understanding it and then there is knowing it directly in our own experiences. Now everyone might not understand Mindfulness as a concept yet. However, each one of us have already experienced Mindfulness without even knowing it.

Just think of a time when you were totally engaged in an

activity, utterly absorbed, you weren't thinking about the bills that is waiting to be paid or about the work that needed to be completed or the to-do list that you needed to close later. Every part of your being was focused in the moment. Maybe you caught your breath at the exquisite sunrise, or may you have experienced it spontaneously when you were watching the beauty of the snow-capped mountains or the mesmerizing beauty of the moon on a full-moon night? Have you then experienced being one with nature? Dancers experience Mindfulness when they lose themselves in the joyful movement of the body and Artist know it when they are absorbed in the art of their creation. When we find ourselves in these moments, a deep sense of connectedness with life suddenly emerges, everything feels alive and pulsating, every pore in us radiates energy and emanates sacredness deep within.

Scientist now concur what Vedic tradition have long been telling us. That the way to fulfilment and true well-being lie not in the external circumstances of our lives, but the internal state of our minds and the quality of our consciousness. Mindfulness in fact is the core-essence of every wisdom and tradition throughout history. It's the reason for every spiritual practice ever performed and more importantly it's the key to true and lasting fulfilment.

Components of Mindfulness

There are three components to Mindfulness—three ways in which our attention shifts gears:

1. On-purpose Attention
2. Being in the present moment
3. Being non-judgmental

Firstly, our attention is held on purpose. Mindfulness involves the conscious and deliberate direction of our awareness. So being mindful, we could say is opposite of being on an Autopilot which unfortunately for so many of us is the normal state of the mind every passing day. And when we are on Autopilot, the mind is noisy. It chatters away ceaselessly and almost constantly. When we practice mindfulness, it allows us to wake-up, out oof the autopilot. It allows us to hold attention where we consciously choose.

The second component of Mindfulness is that we are immersed in the present moment. If we leave our mind to its own defences, it habitually wanders away from the present moment and constantly gets caught up in replaying the past and projecting into the future. In other words, we are very rarely fully in the present moment of our lives. Mindful attention however is completely engaged in the present moment experience. In the here and the now.

Thirdly, when practicing Mindfulness, our attention is held non-judgmentally. We are aiming not to control or suppress our thoughts in anyway. We simply aim to pay attention to our experiences without judging, labelling, or making stories about them in any way. Mindfulness then allows us to become the watcher of the sense, perception, thoughts, and emotions as they arise, without getting caught up in them and being swept away in their current.

When we live mindfully, we can literally transform our entire world from inside-out. And from that place live in harmony with ourselves and live in harmony with the world around us. Dalai Lama says 'The main cause of a happy life is within you.'

Research on Mindfulness

There also have been several studies over the past 10 years that utilise neuroimaging to research the brain morphology and its changes with mindfulness. A meta-analysis performed with the help of twenty-one neuroimaging studies was performed using the brains of 300 experienced mindfulness practitioners.

According to the study, mindfulness and meditation influenced changes in the following eight specific regions of the brain:

1. Rostro-lateral prefrontal cortex
2. Sensory cortices
3. Insular cortex
4. Hippocampus
5. Anterior cingulate cortex
6. Mid-cingulate cortex
7. Superior longitudinal fasciculus
8. Corpus callosum

The study also suggested that people, especially in a workplace have:

- Positive outlook towards work
- Improved attention to detail and quality of focus
- Better interpersonal behaviour with more empathy and compassion towards co-workers
- Better personal relationships
- Boosted stability control and efficacy

Benefits of Mindfulness

Mindfulness has its roots in Buddhism founded about 2,600 years ago. It is however, a highly practised psychotherapeutic approach today. There have been scientific studies and evidence showing benefits of mindfulness in every individual who has undergone training. Theoretically, Mindfulness provides a balanced mind, improved focus, better concentration, self-resilience, emotional intelligence, mental clarity and much more while portraying kindness, compassion, and acceptance.

1. **Enhanced Memory** – A study conducted on a group of people undergoing mindfulness training showed positive results in enhancing 'working memory' capacity. It helped them in performing tasks more efficiently and showed a greater positive effect due to a buffer that is created against losses to 'working memory' capacity. The study also inferred that meditative practices associated with mindfulness also improved the working memory of these individuals.
2. **Reduce Negative Thought Process** – In scientific terminology, mindfulness improves the metacognitive awareness state of every individual. This ensures that you are not involving your feelings into everything that is occurring currently. Such behaviour helps in decreasing negative thinking patterns and creates a positive impact which is necessary to develop healthier coping mechanisms to deal with anxiety and depression.
3. **Reduced Stress, Anxiety, and Depression** – Studies have shown that the contemporary times have witnessed an increase in the deterioration of our

mental health, such as experiencing stress, anxiety, and depression due to our unhealthy personal and professional lives. Mindfulness training can help alleviate the symptoms and cleanse the mind of negative thoughts to establish a balance. Studies performed have provided support to the fact that there are positive neural changes and reactivity seen with the help of mindfulness in subjects that are undergoing mental stress.

4. **Reduced Emotional Reactivity** – Mindfulness positively helps in reducing emotional reactivity which generally springs an uncontrollable reaction to your surroundings. It's a feeling that can take people out of their comfort zone and make them feel victimized. Such a feeling works towards the downfall of individuals and can be a dangerous mindset when it comes to running an organisation.
5. **Relationship Satisfaction** – Since a person becomes better at handling stress with mindfulness, they achieve the capability to resolve relationship stress in a much better way. It also helps them communicate better to their partners or co-workers to achieve a peaceful resolution in case of conflicts.
6. **Adaptive and Problem-Solving Ability** – For organisations looking to build a team that drives them towards profit, they require employees who are adaptive and efficient at work. Mindfulness ensures that individuals can quickly acclimatise to the new projects, situations, and even handle multiple tasks at a time. Since mindfulness helps in clearing the mind

of unwanted clutter, it can improve the problem-solving abilities of individuals as well.

7. **Generate Empathetic Behaviour** – It is important in life for everyone to be empathetic, especially at workplace to ensure that the teams and the organisation work optimally. Empathy generated with the help of mindfulness training helps employees to work better with each other even under stressful conditions.
8. **Other Known Benefits** – Mindfulness is known to play a major role in helping manage subjective pain in individuals. It provides the ability to manage chronic pain to help improve the quality of life. Apart from psychological stress management, individuals are also known to improve their immune system and build better genetic health with the help of mindfulness. Some other benefits of mindfulness are enhanced functionalities of the brain's middle prefrontal lobe area that includes intuition, morality, self-insight, and fear modulation.

Mediation and the Basics of Mindful Meditation Practice

In mindfulness meditation, we learn to pay attention to our breathing patterns, as the air goes in and out and notice when the mind wanders from this task. We also learn how to return to, and remain in, the present moment—to anchor ourselves in the here and now on purpose, without judgement. This practice of returning to the breath builds the muscles of attention and mindfulness.

The idea behind mindfulness seems simple—the practice takes patience. Indeed, renowned meditation teacher Sharon Salzberg recounts that her first experience with meditation showed her how quickly the mind gets caught up in other tasks.

'I thought, okay, what will it be, like, 800 breaths before my mind starts to wander? And to my absolute amazement, it was one breath, and I'd be gone.'

Meditation is exploring. It's not a fixed destination. Your head doesn't become a vacuum, which is free of thoughts, utterly undistracted. It's a special place where each moment is momentous. When we meditate, we venture into the workings of our minds—our sensations (air blowing on our skin or a harsh smell wafting into the room), our emotions (love this, hate that, crave this, loathe that) and our thoughts (wouldn't it be weird to see an elephant playing a trumpet).

Mindfulness meditation asks us to suspend judgment and unleash our natural curiosity about the workings of the mind, approaching our experience with warmth and kindness, to ourselves and others.

Mindfulness is available to us in every moment, whether through meditations and body scans, or mindful moment practices like taking time to pause and breathe when the phone rings instead of rushing to answer it.

Mindfulness helps us put some space between ourselves and our responses, breaking down our conditioned reactions. Here's how to tune into mindfulness throughout the day:

- Set aside sometime – You don't need a meditation

cushion or bench, or any sort of special equipment to access your mindfulness skills, but you need to set aside some time and space.

- Observe the present moment as it is – The aim of mindfulness is not shut the mind off or to attempt to achieve a state of eternal calm. Rather, it is to pay attention to the present moment, without judgment. Easier said than done, we know!
- Let your judgements roll by – When we notice judgements arise during our practice, we can make a mental note of them and let them pass.
- Return to observing the present moment as it is – Our minds often get carried away in thoughts. That's why mindfulness is the practice of returning again and again to the present moment.
- Be kind to your wandering mind – Don't judge yourself for whatever thoughts crop up, just practice recognizing when your mind has wandered off, and gently bring it back.

That's the practice. It's often been said that it's very simple, but it's not necessarily easy. The work is to just keep doing it. Results will accrue.

Meditation focuses on the breath, not because there is anything special about it, but because the physical sensation of breathing is always there, and you can use it as an anchor to the present moment. Throughout the practice you may find yourself caught up in thoughts, emotions, sounds—wherever your mind goes, simply come back again to the next breath. Even if you only come back once, that's alright.

Simple Meditation Practice

Meditation is simpler (and harder) than most people think. Read these steps, make sure you're somewhere where you can relax into this process, set a timer, and give it a shot.

- Sit comfortably. Find a spot that gives you a stable, solid, comfortable seat. Notice what your legs are doing. If on a cushion, cross your legs comfortably in front of you. If on a chair, rest the bottoms of your feet on the floor.
- Straighten your upper body, but don't stiffen. Your spine has a natural curvature. Let it be there.
- Notice what your arms are doing. Situate your upper arms parallel to your upper body. Rest the palms of your hands on any part of your legs where it feels most natural.
- Soften your gaze. Drop your chin a little and let your gaze fall gently downward. It's not necessary to close your eyes. You can simply let what appears before your eyes be there without focussing on it.
- Feel your breath. Bring your attention to the physical sensation of breathing, the air moving through your nose or mouth, the rising and falling of your belly or your chest.
- Notice when your mind wanders from your breath. Inevitably, your attention will leave the breath and wander to other places. Don't worry. There's no need to block or eliminate thinking. When you notice your mind wandering gently return your attention to the breath.

- Be kind about your wandering mind. You may find your mind wandering constantly. That's normal. Instead of wrestling with your thoughts, practice observing them without reacting. Just sit and pay attention. As hard as it is to maintain, that's all there is. Come back over and over again without judgement or expectation.
- When you're ready, gently lift your gaze (if your eyes are closed, open them). Take a moment and notice any sounds in the environment. Notice how your body feels right now. Notice your thoughts and emotions.

That's it! That's the practice. You focus your attention, your mind wanders, you bring it back, and you try to do it as kindly as possible (as many times as you need to).

Benefits associated with Meditation

While meditation isn't a cure-all, it can certainly provide some 'much-needed' space in your life. Sometimes, that's all we need, to make better choices for ourselves, our families, and our communities.

The most important tools you can bring with you to your meditation practice are a little patience, some kindness for yourself, and a comfortable place to sit.

When we meditate, we inject far-reaching and long-lasting benefits into our lives. The bonus would be inessentiality of any extra gear or an expensive membership.

Here are five reasons to meditate:

1. To understand your pain
2. To lower your stress
3. To connect better
4. To improve focus
5. To reduce brain chatter

How to Make Mindfulness a Habit

It's estimated that 95% of our behaviour runs on autopilot. That's because neural networks underlie all our habits, reducing millions of sensory inputs per second into manageable shortcuts so we can function in this world. These default brain signals are so efficient that they often cause us to relapse into old behaviours before we can remember the need of the moment.

Mindfulness is the exact opposite of these default processes. It is executive control rather than autopilot, and enables intentional actions, willpower, and decisions. But that takes practice. The more we activate the intentional brain, the stronger it gets. Every time we do something deliberate and new, we stimulate neuroplasticity, activating our grey matter, which is full of newly sprouted neurons that have not yet been groomed for the 'autopilot' brain.

But here's the problem. While our intentional brain knows what is best for us, our autopilot brain causes us to shortcut our way through life. So how can we coach ourselves to be mindful when we need it the most? This is where the notion of 'behaviour design' comes in. It's a way to put your intentional brain in the driver's seat. There are two ways to do that—first, slowing down the autopilot brain by putting obstacles in its way, and second, removing obstacles in the path of the intentional brain, so it can gain control.

Shifting the balance to give your intentional brain more power takes some work, though. Here are some ways to get started:

- Put on reminders for meditation around you. If you intend to do some yoga or to meditate, put your yoga mat or your meditation cushion in the middle of your floor so you can't miss it as you walk by.
- Refresh your reminders regularly. You may use sticky notes to remind yourself of a new intention. However, since, your autopilot brain and old habits take over after a while, try to write new notes to yourself, add variety or make them funny. That way they'll stick with you longer.
- Create new patterns. You could try a series of 'If this, then that' messages to create easy reminders to shift into the intentional brain. For instance, you might come up with, 'If office door, then deep breath,' to shift into mindfulness as you are about to start your workday. Or 'If phone rings, take a breath before answering.' Each intentional action to shift into mindfulness will strengthen your intentional brain.

Integrating Mindfulness in everyday life

In day-to-day contexts, being mindful also implies paying attention to the consequences of one's actions after paying attention to the actions themselves.

- **Bathing:** Bathing is an excellent time to get in touch with your body and notice it for what it is. Accept and acknowledge the shapes, textures, and bathing sensations for what they really are.
- **Eating:** Mindful eating is a popular approach to experience and enjoy food. Notice the different tastes and mouthfeels. Concentrate on the smell of the food. Pay attention to your portion sizes. Notice the physical act of eating. Understand how you feel when you eat something.
- **Sports:** Regularly practised movements are often automated. However, there are a few movements which we rarely notice. Learn to observe your movements and monitor your breathing to experience an immersive mindful state.
- **Cleaning:** Cleaning demands attention, so being mindful while cleaning could be easier than mindful sports. Use your existing attention to observe and notice dust patterns, wipe marks, and hand movements.
- **Conversations:** Mindful talking and Mindful listening is about paying close attention to what you say and hear. Focus on the words, voice, tone, changes in vocal pitch, pauses between words, body language, facial expressions, etc. While speaking, pause and purposefully choose what you want to say.

You may extrapolate from these and apply mindfulness to hobbies like playing musical instruments, texting, social media, etc. Remember, mindfulness is about paying nonjudgmental close attention to all sensory information and thoughts specific to a context.

Mindfulness during eating, cleaning and bathing can reduce the wandering of our minds, which is usually witnessed when we are at our usual activities.

Inculcating Mindfulness Practices in the Early Years

There is nothing more important in this world now than teaching children mindfulness. Children should be allowed to take in all that is happening around them, without being judgmental. It helps them to steady their minds, and hearts, build compassion and empathy, and enables them to speak and act in a manner that is generous, kind, and compassionate for the wellbeing of everyone around them. At present most people are living a life of chaos, are distracted, and therefore, are gripped in fear or anxiety.

They are not actually living in the moment. So as adults, first one must start practicing mindfulness (in a secular manner). Once it starts, it will show up in all aspects of the individual's life and integrating it into one's daily life through activities will help children at home and those who we work with, to integrate it into their lives as well. For example, before one begins one's meal, one would say a prayer, thank the divine power, and show gratefulness. This is not a religious practice, but a simple way to bring one's focus to the moment, pay attention to the food that one is about to eat, taste it and feel it enrich one's bodies. Often, adults are seen to eat food while watching a film, or in front of the television without even being aware of what and how much food they have consumed. This shows how they are not mindful and hence, are not paying attention to the present.

Mindfulness techniques differ for different age groups. For young children, it is more playful, short timed with repetitions, and can be stretched all day, in small capsules. Mindfulness practices help in stabilizing their hearts and minds by stopping, pausing, feeling and shifting their attention from what they think to how they feel, which is a more sensory experience. This enables the child to develop self-regulation and feel calm.

When one starts mindfulness interventions with little children, one should keep in mind two things:

1. That it is practiced with a child when she/he is not upset and is focused. This helps in developing attention and helps the child to self-regulate. For example, short pauses that may be inserted into their everyday life to pay attention to their feelings or by merging meditation practice with other activities, such as story yoga or sports.
2. Secondly, in a situation where the child is upset or too excited, one needs to help him/her STOP, PAUSE, and shift his/her attention from the immediate issue to a more PHYSICAL experience like breathing—slow breathing to be precise.

Mindfulness practices should be a natural part of the child's daily life, just like brushing one's teeth or combing one's hair. It may be introduced in small capsules during the day and gradually incorporated into every moment of one's life. Parents and educators, need to practice mindfulness so that they become role models for the children.

Mindfulness Techniques that may be introduced as activities with children

There are a lot of benefits including mindfulness activities for pre-schoolers. These help them develop self-awareness and self-regulation skills.

- **Movement-based mindfulness activities:**
  Children love to move! It is their natural state. So, if mindfulness activities are combined with movement, they will lead to greater engagement.
  - **Nature Walks**: Children go out for short walks and while walking, observe with attention all the things they come across, the sounds, the wind, how the ground feels, what the weather is like, without putting so much thought into them, simply observing and paying attention as they walk along. This activity will help them to be more aware and observant of their surroundings.
  - **Flying like a bird**: This is a fantastic activity where children are made to combine movement with deep breathing. When they lift their hands assuming them to be wings, they breathe in. Similarly, when they slowly bring their hands down, they breathe out.
  - **Animal Dancing**: This activity helps children to let loose their pent-up emotions and stress. The team leader is made to choose an animal card (for example they pick a monkey) and everyone goes around the space, hooting and swinging their arms.

Sensory based mindfulness activities:

- Children need to practice **mindful eating** i.e., chewing food slowly and experiencing the sensation of the food in their mouths. This activity will help them to awaken their taste buds and enhance their sense of flavour and enjoy the moment. Blindfolded fruit tasting game helps children use taste and touch to savour the moment.
- Another remarkably interesting exercise is **feeling with the feet on the bottom of the floor**. This is a wonderful grounding experience. Walking on the grass that has droplets of morning dew is another activity that incredibly connects one to the present moment.
- **Blindfolded activities like touch and tell** help in developing mindfulness. Children find such activities very interesting and at the same time, it helps them awaken their senses and stay mindful. With the sense of sight temporarily switched off by a blindfold, the other senses are heightened. Therefore, the player can experience enhanced concentration levels during the moment.
- **Breathing activities** help children to stay calm and relaxed. It is a wonderful tool to control one's emotions.

Some other activities:

- **Worry Dolls**: Worry dolls are a fantastic idea that originated in Guatemala. They are small figures that a child is supposed to put under his/her pillow at night and when they wake up, his/her worries are gone. Children enjoy making their own worry dolls. One can make a really simple one by using a stick and winding wool or other materials around it.

- **Positive Affirmations for Children**:
  Affirmations are not only for adults. Children can benefit from using positive affirmations too to foster a mindset of optimism and success. Positive affirmations can develop creative thinking, build self-esteem and create a growth mindset.

Allow children to share their experiences, involve them in discussions and decision-making processes and talk to them as well as listen to their thoughts. These small moments of awareness give the child a grounding and steadying effect.

Benefits of Mindfulness Practices for children

Although an ample amount of data is present showing how adults reflect the positive impact of mindfulness practice, its impact on children has not been researched upon much. However, the little data that is available appear to be promising and show positive changes in children in their early years.

A series of studies published in the *Psychological Assessment* by Greco et al. in 2011 argue that mindfulness is positively correlated to quality of life, academic competence, and social skills. A review in *The Journal of Children's Services* in 2013 states that regular practise of mindfulness improves one's mental well-being, mood, self-esteem, positive behaviour, and even academic learning. Below are listed a few benefits of mindfulness:

- Mindfulness practices help children to have greater control over their emotions, improve mental and physical health and their overall well-being.
- It has been shown to reduce stress, anxiety, bad behaviour, reactivity.
- Improves self-esteem, self-awareness, empathy, brings greater calmness and relaxation.
- Mindfulness helps in enhancing cognitive skills, performance skills, and executive functions.
- Improves concentration, focus, memory, innovative thinking, and reasoning skills.
- Improves ability to work in a team and enables conflict resolution.

> 'Every human being has the capacity to be mindful, so it is not something strange. We all have a seed of mindfulness in us. If we keep practicing, that seed will grow strong, and any time we need it, the energy of mindfulness will be there for us.'
>
> **Zen Master Thich Nhat Hanh**
>
> *Practicing Mindfulness with Children*

REFERENCES:

Mindful Staff, "The Science of Mindfulness." mindful, August 31, 2022. https://www.mindful.org/the-science-of-mindfulness/

Edmunds, Ellis. "Mindful Therapy for Anxiety-Rockbridge, Oakland, CA." August 29, 2018. Video, www.drellisedmunds.com

"Mindfulness for Kids." mindful. https://www.mindful.org/mindfulness-for-kids/

MANDY WORSLEY & JULIE ROBINSON
Co-founders of Mini Minds Matter, United Kingdom

Mandy and Julie have many years of health, well-being, and business experience. Julie is a successful early-years business owner with over 50 staff members and Mandy has a background of 26 years in the NHS.

SIX

THE POWER OF POSITIVE SELF-TALK

Julie Robinson and Mandy Worsley

Trust your inner-creator and let go of your inner-critic.

J.R. Incer

Mastering Success: The Key to Self-Empowerment and Higher Consciousness.

IN LIFE, we are never alone. Our days are narrated by our inner voice and our activities are accompanied by self-talk. Sometimes, this is helpful and convivial, but mostly it's destructive, negative and unproductive.

What is self-talk?

Self-talk is defined as talks or thoughts directed at ourselves. It's the internal conversation that accompanies us throughout our day.

That self-talk, we all have inside, can be the internal voice of our daily lives, or the inner critic commentating on everything we do, or on occasions the sole celebrator of our accomplishments.

As adults we have the ability to recognise whether this self-talk is negative in nature or positive, whether it's helpful or is a hindrance. Despite recognising it, we can still be a slave to our self-doubts and lack the skills or understanding of how to navigate through the unhelpful sound. We can sometimes find it challenging to be more optimistic and move away from a destructive thought process that encapsulates us. This is sometimes through habit forming, the more we respond negatively the more our brains are wired to be negative.

Yet it wasn't like this when we were in the womb, or a young child. This is a behaviour we tend to learn and develop over time which can be self-limiting, destructive, and often, at the very least, unhelpful. We all know that, as babies, we fail to understand negativity. A baby attempts to crawl, it fails initially and yet, it keeps trying. Its motivation is to move, as it is not aware that failing exists. It then attempts to walk; but again, falls down repeatedly. However, eventually it finds a solution, whether it uses a piece of furniture for support. It eventually succeeds.

As children grow, they are influenced by adults around them and their inner voice starts to waken. So how do we support them to challenge that inner voice? As adults, carers and educators, our role is to teach children early on, so they can be equipped with a set of skills for life.

Language, in this case needs to be more positive around children. It is best to make things as playful as possible to help balance out the unhelpful habits they have formed or are beginning to form. Dr Dan Sigel explains in his book *The Whole Brain Child*, suggesting children's brains can be explained to children in a fun and imaginative way. He likens the brain to a house. The house has an upstairs and a downstairs. He suggests that children can imagine characters inside their houses which allows them to control who they are and what they say. He also explains this concept by informing them that frontal lobe of the brain houses the emotional, problem solving and rational characters. However, worry and fear lives in the lower part of the brain. Once the quiet voice starts to make itself known, first and foremost, it is difficult to identify that something has changed inside the house. The louder the voice grows from the inner critic, the more our brain induces fear and anxiety in us. However, children need to be able to recognise what the positive inner critic sounds like compared to the negative one.

Why do we need to ensure self-talk is positive?

The practice of self-talk, is also known as self-care. We teach our children to develop skills to get more independent with age, starting from teaching them how to brush their teeth, get dressed etc. Similarly, self-talk is another way of improving your child's independence and life skills. Teaching and supporting self-care are basically childcare. Self-care and self-awareness are what gives us the ability to consciously respond to our environment and thus, organize our emotions and thoughts. The main aspect is being aware of what you are doing, what you are thinking and what you want to achieve. It is influenced by your subconscious mind, and it reveals your thoughts, beliefs, questions, and ideas.

However, self-talk can be both negative and positive. It can be encouraging, and it can be distressing. Much of your self-talk depends on pessimism. Positive thinking and optimism can be effective stress management tools. Indeed, having a more positive outlook on life can provide you with some health benefits. For example, a study conducted in 2010 shows that optimists have a better quality of life (Brene Brown).

If you believe your self-talk is too negative, or if you want to emphasise positive self-talk, you can learn to shift that inner dialogue. It can help you to be a more positive person, and it may improve your health.

So how can we achieve this? Does self-talk make our children happy?

Firstly, as parents, we have to be the role model by providing affirmations, then teach how to convert negative self-talk into positive. It is about identifying when you do it and responding saying that and then repeating it to something positive.

Help your children rephrase their negative emotions into positive alternatives. They can do it in the form of a conversation with themselves or positively motivating themselves.

Positive self-talk is a coping skill. It helps to develop positive thinking and eventually develop a child's self-esteem. It can also help to build resilience in a child. By training the brain to think positive repeatedly, leads to an improved outlook in life.

An example of a child in negative self-talk, maybe when a child says 'I can't do this' or 'I am no good at this!' At this moment the child is expressing fear or anxiety about a new situation, or one they have not exceeded at earlier. They experience and display lack of self-esteem as a result of self-doubt. In order to fight this fear and anxiety, the very thought building this fear must be challenged. Therefore, incorporation of self-affirmations in one's daily life must be encouraged. Thus, statements like, 'There is no such thing as can't only can,' 'I believe in myself and can achieve anything I want to' should be advised to remind oneself everday.' The use of affirmations regularly reinforces this practice. Positive affirmations are one of the best ways to get children involved in saying positive things. You may ask them to write their own affirmations and to come up with ideas of what to say, to control their inner critic and build new pathways in their brain. If you walk to school, maybe try jumping on certain flags stones and then you have to shout affirmations. 'I am amazing,' 'I am brave,' 'I am bright.'

However, it is clear that those who are more positive and use more positive self-talk are more likely to have a growth mindset, take risks and enjoy learning, therefore, achieving their full potential.

Setting the scene for success in children through the use of self-talk and growth mindset.

In order for parents to understand the Growth Mindset, let's first look at what this means for you and your child. How you think—whether the locus of your thoughts is fixated on a specific object at a certain point of time or on multiple possibilities define your mindset—precisely into two kinds, i.e., growth mindset and fixed mindset.

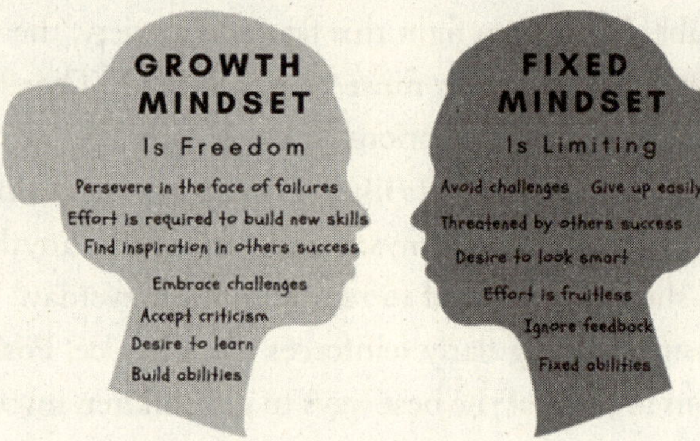

Image from *Upgrade your mindset* by Vinita Bansal.

'In a growth mindset, people believe that their most basic abilities can be developed through dedication and hard work—brains and talent are just the starting point. This view creates a love of learning and a resilience that is essential for great accomplishment (Dweck, 2015).'

Having a growth mindset is essential to your happiness, achievement at work, and success in life. Those with a fixed mindset believe that intelligence, talent and abilities are only in those who are born with it.

Science tells us that the period from the conception of a foetus to the age of five is crucial. Throughout this period the brain develops exponentially and experiences lay down the foundations of the skills, knowledge and confidence that helps young children to navigate future challenges and realise their full potential. This means children in their early years are especially receptive to experiences that promote development of motor, cognitive, language, social, and self-regulation skills. When children do not experience adequate care, attention and love, this can lead to poor outcomes, both physical and mental.

Scientific evidence shows that the development of our brains during the first 18 months of life is faster than any other period of growth. However, studies published by The Royal Foundation Centre for Early Childhood, set up by the Duchess of Cambridge have inferred that one in three parents are not aware of this, and hence, might not cultivate the necessary habits which can create a better impact on the child's future.

A significant proportion of parents in the UK of children from 0–5-year-olds (69%) underestimate the importance of the early years. This contrasts with the scientific evidence which is clear on the primacy of the early years in providing the foundation for both children's future development and their life choices as adults.

There is a significant gap in understanding of how rapidly the brain develops during the most critical first two years. Studies conducted state that these gaps could result in less active interaction with children in the early years, particularly before the child starts to exhibit outward signs of development, such as speaking. It may also lead to a more 'passive' approach to caring for children, focusing on physical needs rather than their emotional and social development. To increase understanding of how the brain develops, we need to translate and increase accessibility of developmental science, so that parents, future parents and the society can acknowledge the importance of active interaction with children. Interactive parenting and positive role models lead to a more positive mindset and willingness and motivation to learn.

Having a growth mindset is a critical element in your happiness, achievement at work and success in life. It's important to use both a growth mindset and positive self-talk to support children on their learning journey from the earliest of days. This is because of the impact it has on their development and their willingness to take risks, try new things, and ultimately achieve.

Name:...

GROWTH MINDSET
What Can I Say to Myself?

Instead of…	Try thinking…
I'm not good at this.	What am I missing?
I'm awesome at this.	I'm on the right track.
I give up.	I'll use some of the strategies we've learned.
This is too hard.	This may take some time and effort.
I can't make this any better.	I can always keep trying to improve.
I just can't do math. (or reading, or social studies, or writing, or science…)	I'm going to train my brain in math. (or reading, or social studies, or writing, or science…)
I made a mistake.	Mistakes help me to learn better.

This image can be used to help you and your child to change the way they use world language every day. Use this to practise and teach children how to use positive language. Growth Mindset What to Say?
Uploaded by **Dallas Anne Thompson**

If we can allow parents to understand their child's brain and their own, in this easy and fun way, then they can start to understand why they feel a certain way, why they react to certain things and how they can change unwanted reactions, emotions and feelings in themself and their child. By calming their Activas Urus mind, using daily affirmation and meditation, they are on the right track to a happier and healthier life, building towards a growth mindset.

Is Success about learning? Does a growth mindset have an impact?

One thing we as parents focus on is the success of our children. How do we measure success—is it a great job or our children earning the best money or being the best academic? Well, this notion of success is how society deems it. However, if children display self-doubt and lack of self-worth, it will always limit them in achieving any success. Surely, we want our children to belief in themselves and have strong disposition in life. We want our children to get up if they fall and try to keep going. We help them to understand that we learn from failing, from our failures. Catherine Miner (2019) says that self-perception is key to a successful life. It's about how you think and feel about yourself, not what others think and want for you. She also provides us with words that should never be used.

These words include never, can't, won't, hate, want, might. She adds that words are so powerful that they can change a whole sentence and lead to negative thoughts and negative self-talk. As adults we would find avoiding these words challenging, for a child even more so.

To grow your mindset, Carol Dweck (2017) says, 'People are born with a love of learning. Even if you think something is difficult you can still plunge yourself into it wholeheartedly.' Therefore, picture your brain forming new connections and see yourself achieving what you desire, don't fear the challenges and more importantly take a risk.

When things go right and self-talk is positive, it can be successful. Let's look at the Polgar family. They have produced three of the most successful chest players. The youngest is the best female chess player of all time. So how did all the three children achieve so well? We could argue if it is in the genes. However, it is more likely passed down through mindset. Dweck (2019) suggests that the father used and applied a growth mindset to everything. The growth mindset lets people use and develop their minds fully, they are not focused on limiting thoughts, or lack self-esteem or belonging and do not let other people define them.

We know that everyone is capable of having a growth mindset, according to 'Dweck' but we have to understand we are not innately perfect and at times may slip back to that inner critical voice and fixed mindset.

As carers and educators, we now understand the power of the word. We understand that we all have that inner critic to hold us back. However, we cannot allow our children to be influenced by a negative mindset. We want our children to experience challenges and maybe failure in order to know and understand what real mental, self-worth and hard work is.

According to Miner (2019), we are not meant to stay in one place like rocks, but to flow like rivers. We grow ourselves, spread our wings and achieve, growth and change will keep evolving. Koplewicz (2021) says that parents should scaffold around the child but never impede or block whatever shape it is taking—a parent's role is to form a scaffold around their child and maintain quality control. So long as we support our children daily in achieving their true potential, help them cope with change and support them in building inner strength, they are more likely to have a can-do attitude to life.

Now that you have a better idea of how your inner thoughts work, it's time to switch gears and learn a new approach to self-talk. Look back at some of the thoughts you may have had and reword them in a kinder, more positive light.

How to Use Positive Self-Talk for children to Overcome Anxiety

Use positive statements in the house daily. Things like, you are going to have a good day today. I bet you can't wait to sit that test and show how amazing you are. Have a feelings checker, so if you are feeling a little more frustrated that day, you may need to use talk more that day. If you are feeling angry, try to meditate or breathe slower, tell yourself 'I am calm'.

Try to find ways to encourage laughter in the house, tell a joke day, say a poem, or pull a funny face. We know laughter sends the right endorphins to feel good.

Try to surround yourself with positive people, you may notice that positive feedback enlightens you and makes you strive for more. Negativity brings your mood down, and the feeling of not worthy or good enough starts to come forwards and take a hold.

Seeing positive words can redirect your thoughts, so put

one on the fridge, or on your mirror and do the same for your children. It forms good habits and trains the brain to be positive.

A practical guide on how to use these tools in the nursery setting to build stronger parent partnerships and outcomes for children (setting the tone for learning and adventure).

Activities to do to set positive self-talk and mindset:

- Mindful Meditation

  How to do: Set your routine accordingly, so that you can find a quiet space, choose an appropriate time to meditate.

  Why do it?

  Meditation helps to quieten the mind and take control of random thoughts. It allows you to just be aware of what is happening in the moment. Meditation helps children respond to internal signals of stress before their brains give in to those fear feelings of stress and anxiety. It allows for that quiet time in nursery or pre-school.

- Massage: This could be a hand massage.

  How to do: Get the children to do peer on peer hand massage. They could use a nursery rhyme or poem like 'round and round the garden'.

  Why do it?

  This allows children to connect with each other and identify how this feeling helps them to relax.

- Mindful smelling
  In nursery or pre-school, use mindful smelling during circle time. It could help children identify objects? Closing their eyes, smelling an orange or a lemon, or coffee or tea or a flower—it is a great way to connect with one of their senses in a calm controlled way.

A practical guide on how to use these tools in the home to enhance your child's mental wellbeing and happiness. Focus on connection and bonding.

- Mindful Meditation
  What Should I do?
  It may be a good idea to do this when your children return from school. It can allow them to reset their mind and thoughts.
  Why do it?
  It helps with the process of self-awareness. It can help the child deal better with their emotions. It also helps reduce stress hormones and improved health, better sleep and improved self-esteem.

- Massage
  What should I do?
  After a bath, ask your child to lay down and use rapeseed oil, or coconut oil, use swirling motions on the back, you could incorporate a story massage using finger tips for the rain, brush strokes for the clouds and circle motion for the sun. Use your imagination to create a story.

Why do it?
Each gentle stroke will reinforce love and connection with your child. It helps their breathing to slow down and get into a calm state of mind. It can also strengthen your bond and help you recognise their needs and improve sleep.

Mindful smelling
Encourage your child to be involved in cooking with you, be it smelling the herbs and spices or smell the flowers in the garden. It is another great way to bond with your child and allow them to figure out what they can smell and how it makes them feel.

In the education early years sector, Eagley School House has been using the mini minds approach designed by Julie Robinson and Mandy Worsley, for over a year, to support children after COVID. It has displayed a significant impact in the children aged two to five years. Below are some examples of case studies from children.

Child A with Special educational needs: Visually impaired

Child A, his nursery education at a new school during the first wave of the pandemic. His former school was shut down due to COVID because of which he was at home for some time. During this period, he could not meet any expectations, be it personal, social or emotional. Hence, during our sessions, he would always hold back from activities. During the day he would often hit himself and say negative sentences about himself. He was averse to risk taking and worried about playing outdoors. Parents reported he would also hold back in other situations, for example, in visiting the park or other areas and be afraid to access any equipment in the park. On one occasion mother reported that he would not access the stairway to the slide. He got frustrated and upset. Mother said that she had to help him as he said he couldn't do it. We held a meeting with mother and decided to try and use more positive language around him. We tried to support him by saying positive affirmations and words. Due to setting up such early intervention with parents, we started to notice a change in his behaviour. Over the next ten to twelve months, we consistently used mindfulness techniques to help regulation, daily affirmations and positive self-talk to help 'child A' learn to say positive statements about himself. After months of training, in Jan 2022, when I complimented him on doing so well, he replied enthusiastically, 'That's because I am amazing'. Not only did he have a positive response, his demeanour and posture were upright—confident and proud. He is now ready and willing to take those risks and does not worry about failing.

Child B

He started Eagley School House at the age of two. He had always achieved his milestones but tended to be easily excited and spontaneous. During the pandemic, his parents, like most others wanted to him to stay inside the premises of the house. As the lockdown was slowly lifted, he transformed into a different little boy. He was more wary of new situations and grew cautious about coming back to the Nursery.

It could be seen that his personal and emotional skills and self-confidence had been impacted. After introducing mindful moments, mediations, positive affirmation daily we began to see those improvements in his relationships with others. On one occasion we were learning about being strong, and resilient. He then went home to his father, and as he was working on the garden. He said, 'I know you are strong here, but you need to be strong in here' and pointed to his head. This young boy had an understanding in his own way of why being strong and resilient helps you achieve. The affirmations daily of 'I am strong because...' definitely guided him and another six months on, this boy was achieving, taking risks building friendships, and learning resilience. The parents have worked alongside the setting, carrying out the mini mindful sessions at home and reading the meditations about self-belief designed by Mini Minds Matter UK. This surely demonstrates that educators and parents can make a difference by working together.

Encouraging self-talk and the ideas in this chapter, working collaboratively, the Nursery was able to see many changes in children's self-confidence and resilience. It gave the child continuity of care between home and school, and ensure easy transitions between the two. Working in this way helps parents understand the power positive mindset and talk on developmental learning helping the child reach their full potential and thrive.

REFERENCES

Dweck, Carol S. *Mindset: The New Psychology of Success.* Ballantine Books, 2007.

Cordova, Esther Pia. *Growth Mindset Activities for Kids: 55 Exercises to Embrace Learning and Overcome Challenges.* Rockbridge Press, 2020.

Hoskins, S. *Growth Mindset for Teachers.* Sage Publications, 2019.

Miner, C. *The 30-day self-perception Makeover.* Independently Published, 2019.

Robinson, Julie. *Mini Mindful Moments with Wellasarus and Friends (Mini Minds Matter).* Independently Published, 2021.

SIMRAN BALLANI
Doctorate Student at EIU, Paris, a happiness Coach at Berkeley & Happiitude, Pedagogical Director of CCE Finland

Simran is an Educationist and Workplace Happiness Coach with a career spanning the early beginnings in Education, Talent Management, and Client Servicing for APAC and US markets. In the last 25 years, she has gained many skills that fall outside the traditional genre of Pedagogy & Client Servicing. Currently, she is enjoying her stint with CCE Finland as Pedagogical Director and Communication Head.

SEVEN

ETIQUETTE LEARNING & PUBLIC SPEAKING (ELPS) IN EARLY YEARS

ALTHOUGH THERE have been years of research on the importance of early childhood development and how it lays the foundation of our adult life, very little attention has been paid in studying and investigating how similar experiences and introduction of soft skills in children can be effective in shaping their lives. In this study, the author seeks to examine two different yet co-related studies to determine how experiences of a child's formative years, whether at home or school along with training in soft skills, impact their adulthood in terms of shaping their attitude towards life and leadership. The author shall undertake qualitative research to understand this approach to a child's development.

Drawing on a decade of research and working with teachers, Simran Ballani has developed the ELPS, a unique approach to inculcating etiquette learning and public speaking as part of the academic and home-schooling curriculum. This ELPS approach is an integral part of an innovative approach to early years, offering educators/parents/caregivers a wide range of play way methods on embedding these essential social skills in the early years. By blending two studies, this research aims to explore all early years educators concerned with embedding soft skills, mannerism, instilling confidence and enhancing social interactions of their pupils in early years and building lifelong learners and global citizens.

Simran was intrigued by the world of children, and began studying their early years' experiences when she was blessed with her daughter Sera. She started studying the milestones of ECE in order to make a difference in parenting, in her daughter's life and in the world at large.

A parent's educational attainment of early years development can have a direct correlation to the environment they create for their children and can predict a child's cognitive and behavioural outcome. This led the author to complete her diploma in early childhood education and thus, began her research in the field of early years' experience and development of etiquette learning curriculum.

Here, two studies look at how most experiences in those early years affect life years/decades later from different angles. Many of us might not remember our 1–3 years of childhood, but some profound experiences stick around us for years and continue to influence us positively or negatively in our adulthood.

The first study presented here analyses one of the first groups of students who enrolled in ELPS, tracking their achievements from kindergarten to the 2nd grade in school.

These children have shown some remarkable progress in terms of social interactions, self-esteem, confidence and public speaking as a result of continuous reinforcements and positive experiences within the institution of the family and outside of it.

The second study reflects on the journeys of a few iconic leaders' by zooming in their early years. These leaders have achieved great academic success, have learnt to manage themselves, handled peer pressure, made the right choices, and thus, grew into industry leaders. This study therefore, attempts to show that children raised with knowledge to cultivate independence, discipline, etiquettes in supportive and caring environments tend to do better in life.

1. Theoretical Background

In the modern society, etiquette is the most valued characteristic in a human. It enables us to govern our thoughts and actions and is a polite reminder that we should consider simple ways to defuse the language in which we express our views, make it more reasonable and mould it with politeness. The etiquette that we learn helps us in showing respect towards other people's emotions and feelings.

'Research has shown that half of a person's intelligence is developed by the age of four. Therefore, early childhood interventions can have a lasting effect on intellectual capacity, personality, and social behaviour. Integrated programs that target children in their very early years are therefore, critical for their mental and psychosocial development.' Investment in early child education can increase the return on investment in their later education by making that education more effective. It can also enable participants to earn more and can raise their productivity in the workforce.

Statement of the Problem

Most students are not exposed to or trained in matters of business protocol and etiquette. Furthermore, manners are identified as a job selection attribute and considered important by campus recruiters. Research indicates that many top executives believe that some of the problems in an organization are a result due of lack of knowledge and skills of proper business etiquette. For example, it is estimated that 12% of recent MBA students have proper etiquette skills compared to 40% of mid-management level and 88% of senior-level managers. Further study indicates that members of the younger generation lack competency in etiquette skills. A study shows that over 43% of responding business professionals believed that business etiquette skills of college graduates had gotten worse over the last decade.

Research also indicates that a moment of rudeness is reported to decrease a doctor's performance by more than 50% in an exercise involving a hypothetical life-or-death situation. Seven out of ten employees reported rudeness in the workplace as the number one reason for their unhappiness and resignations. However, the majority of people do not give much importance to the idea that manners, etiquette training and anything that is branded as soft skills can actually contribute to profit and image of the company. Furthermore, we see how lack of empathy, cultural awareness and good manners was not only overlooked but were hidden behind a culture of reporting that started from the top and completely took the HUMAN factor out of the Human Resources department.

Significance of Study

Experiences of Early years and most importantly etiquettes learnt in these formative years have a direct impact on higher studies, job success, parenting and leadership. Numerous studies have shown that early years experiences or struggles have long lasting impact into adulthood and therefore, can affect academic journey, career choices and happiness.

Similarly, various researchers have pointed out that children as young as 18 months can learn simple manners like saying 'Thank You' and 'Please' when reminded even though they might not understand the reason behind it.

Sera was exposed to ELPS via home-schooling around the age of two. The author developed several approach in educating Sera—she conducted playful sessions, such as role plays to ensure understanding of basic etiquettes, responsible behaviour and enhancing confidence, In doing so, she explained the significance of public speaking and encouraged the same as an important aspect of Sera's education. Her family and school also created a supporting and nurturing environment.

Families can set excellent examples by role playing, when it comes to teaching good manners to children and managing their daily lives through the use of dolls, toys and puppets. It was a fun way to let Sera manage the house and pretend play where she serves food. Occasions such as family gathering, simple family meal, vacations, visit to grocery store or restaurant were good social opportunities to instil good manners and make a habitual part of Sera's life in young years, adolescence and beyond. The Merchant Navy background of her grandfather was helpful in instilling discipline in her.

When it comes to chores and personal hygiene, the author has come across several parents of teenagers who constantly complain, 'My children just don't listen and refuse to do chores!' This reaffirms the author's beliefs that each family member's core responsibility is to do their fair share of the chores, be it the dishes, watering the plants or working around in the kitchen. It's a good idea to instil the value early on 'my home my chores' where every family member is a part of running the household and each one plays their fair share in the execution of the task with peace, love and harmony.

Next step was to introduce Sera to one of the core etiquettes of table manners. It was important for her to learn appropriate behaviour, respect food and healthy eating habits. Like with anything else, there were clear family agreements, repetition and reinforcements. This was one of the most important elements to build her social skills. Role play such as making her soft toys to have dinner together went a long way to understand table set up and manners.

Sera being a bit of a shy child, public speaking was introduced to encourage her participation in events with confidence. It improved Sera's overall communication skills, increased her self-esteem and confidence. She evolved in expressing her ideas in front of her class and teachers. This further encouraged her to plan and organise her thoughts and develop her leadership skills.

It was her dad, who spotted Sera's melodious voice and singing. It soon became his mission to bring her out of her shell and help develop confidence in her to sing in front of an audience. Professional vocal training along with various role plays and encouragement has helped Sera build that confidence.

The early years' experience and reinforcement has had a drastic impact on her ability to maintain relationships, empathise with others, cooperate, develop patience and learn how to interact with others. Her journey consisted of developing problem solving skills, being assertive and not shy away to ask for help, being respectful to one self and other positive values. She has also worked on developing her socio emotional skills. From a very shy toddler, to a confident person, in 2022, Sera performed in front of an audience of 1500 above in her school concert without any fear or shyness.

4.1 Importance of Starting Etiquette Learning/ Soft Skills learning at Preschool Level

Imparting soft skills training at the kindergarten level can have a long-term effect on a child's social behaviour which in turn can contribute to professional success once they are ready to face the recruitment committee and the global job markets.

Hebei Teacher's University presented a study in September 2014. The study excerpt is as follows:

> Etiquette is an ethical code of conduct. Etiquette education tells us how to develop civilised habits. If you see a teacher and ignore or enter a room without knocking or open a parcel etc. are some signs of etiquette distaste. Instead of someone else making us understand the etiquette aversion—it's best to master etiquette, harmonious interpersonal relationships etc. during one's lifetime. Early childhood is the best of the early development of intelligence; it is an important period to develop good habits and etiquette education.

This study is further supported by Hebei Teacher's University, Hebei, Shijiazhuang.

Another very important study indicates that positive early experiences promote optimal development of the brain which in turn impacts all areas of development such as emotional, physical, social, cognitive and language. Both social and emotional development influences all other areas of development.

4.2 Importance of Public Speaking in Early Years

Public speaking is a crucial skill to have in today's competitive age. More importantly in a corporate environment-excellent communication skills, communication skills, including being articulate and eloquent is extremely important to achieve success.

Early childhood is the best time to cultivate skills such as dramatics, vocal variations and presenting in front of an audience. Early childhood educators have to work hard to educate and encourage the development of public speaking in pre-schoolers.

5. Research Methodology

During early childhood education experiences are everything. Children will learn manners, etiquettes, core life values and public speaking if they see it in action in their surroundings. These core life skills to be a global citizen can be embedded either by doing or experiencing life skills in reality and also in the form of role-plays, as part of kindergarten curriculum or directly through their own experiences of witnessing in their families-specially both parents. Early years do have impact on our achievements. Taking this idea as basis the for the two studies, the author aims to explore how it does so.

The qualitative research in the second study done via interviews tracks the patterns of all leadership qualities i.e., self-management, social etiquette, credibility, integrity, independence, relationship building abilities, exhibit empathy, and humility. They are confident in empowering the team and also exhibit care for it. They are authentic, constant and consistent and eventually have become role models not only to their close ones but also to society in general.

6. Findings of the Initial Study

Public Speaking

While conducting a study in a school, we asked students in each class to list down their favourite topics with help from the class/course facilitator. We also asked the students to prepare answers for the following, as a part of our research:

- What do they wish their topic to be about?
- Why did they like it?
- What was so good about it?

- How does it help to enhance their knowledge on the subject?
- How will they like to share their viewpoint with their class?

We used a similar exercise to incorporate etiquette learning—firstly by adding some polite words such as 'Please' and 'Thank You' amongst other words—simple but necessary. Furthermore, the activity involved training and educating them with social mannerism, restaurant manners, table manners, expressing gratitude etc.

We learned that the early childhood years are the absolute grass root level of observation, curiosity and absorption. This is a perfect time to imbibe this crucial social learning and public speaking. Upon interviewing 30 parents on the impact of etiquette learning and public speaking on their children,

90% of them were able to submit their written testimony/progression on the changes they observed in their child's overall social interaction, over the course of the academic year. Children were greeting their friends and family, used mannerisms for social interactions and there was significant demonstration of their etiquette learning in their day-to-day communication with whoever they engaged with.

7. Observing the ongoing impact (2019–2022)

Author tracked the ongoing lives of five children and interviewed their parents. These children seem to have shown recognizable influence of etiquette learning curriculum. There is a significant change in terms of how children have learnt to present themselves, overcome stage fright and depict good mannerism.

This research has evolved from children learning basic etiquettes via role plays to overcoming stage fright for good. This in turn also ensured equal opportunity to all children, irrespective of their home or social environment. Most of the children these days come from nuclear families and parents find it difficult to impart this crucial social skill training at home. Kindergarten's inclusive curriculum of ELPS has helped in training children in etiquette and public speaking. This curriculum provides each child an enriching experience of self-expression, encouraging children to educate themselves on topics such as waste management, recycling and learning about the rich culture of India. Children, as a result gain confidence to present on these topics during monthly assemblies, which can be an enriching experience for these young learners.

Parent's feedback indicates that children became less dependent, were able to do simple chores, became better at human interaction including being more polite and respectful to diverse cultures and have learnt basic table manners, etc. Such learning as a part of the ongoing kindergarten curriculum and reinforcement at home has enhanced children's socio-emotional development. Here are ongoing observations shared by some parents who were interviewed in the period March to December 2022.

8. Findings of the Ongoing Study

Naithan Lowell - Age 8 Years

'Naithan over the years has developed into a very confident person, and whether it is a class activity or a competition, he volunteers for it without hesitation or stage fear. He is extremely active, brave, sharing and caring, collaborating and cooperating while respecting boundaries. He is grateful for his early learning of ELPS and puts all his learning into today's activity and his actions'.

Abraham Lowell - Father of Naithan

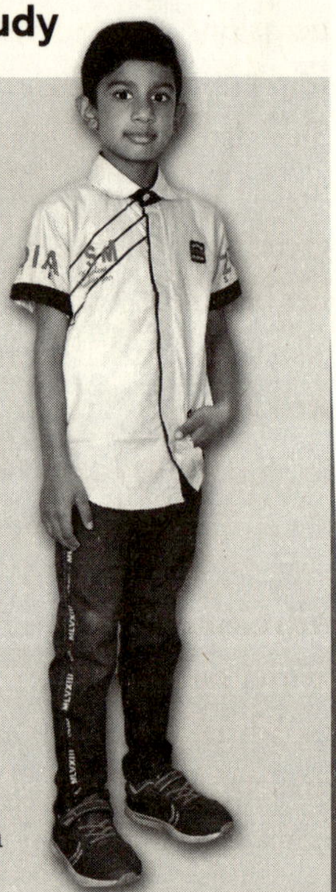

Arohi Sinha - Age 8 Years

'The ELPS (Etiquette Learning & Public Speaking) curriculum introduced in pre-school was really great for Arohi. In the last couple of years, we have seen tremendous growth in Arohi in various spheres. Her confidence has increased a lot while talking to the elders, performing stage shows, etc. She has performed shows on the stage on various occasions and has received due appreciation. We were also impressed with the growth in the contents of her vocabulary. She also learned basic etiquette which helped her to grow in the right direction, respecting her peers and elders, and greeting them whenever she meets them. She keeps sharing her belongings with her friends and shows care for them. She also keeps herself clean and maintains basic hygiene. Arohi is well known in her primary school due to her confidence and good manners.'

Mr. Khem and Mrs. Gargi, parents of Arohi

Advaith Anil - Age 7 Years

We witnessed rapid development in Advaith's personality in 2019 due to the impact of the ELPS curriculum. It is very evident how Advaith's socialising skills improved. ELPS really helped to reveal what he is capable of. We no longer see him shying away or being scared to perform on the stage. We still see the ongoing impact if he has to greet someone socially or visit a restaurant and depict his table manners. I am very happy to see how my son has improved leaps and bounds due to the introduction of public speaking training.

Hetaaksh Reddy, Age 9 Years

'My son Hetaaksh was very shy, but the ELPS curriculum built in him a lot of confidence, as a result of which he can do anything without fear. Small little things make a big difference in our lives. He started to greet everyone and treat himself and others with respect. He believes in the power of reuse, reduce & recycle. Gradually, he started helping in the kitchen and with other work at home these small things made a big difference. ELPS was a welcome addition which instilled such good etiquette in our kids, teaching them how to speak and treat others with respect.'

—Ms Namita, mother of Hetaaksh

Sera Ballani, Age 10 Years

'Sera has evolved into a very confident and emotionally intelligent child as a result of ELPS. To mention, she was initially shy and would be a bit apprehensive while speaking on a stage. But instilling etiquette learning & public speaking skills as a family, we witnessed significant changes in her. She is now more respectful, responsible, confident and yet empathetic. Sera can now perform on the stage, be it performing a dance or a song without any hesitation or fear. She has undertaken vocal training for the last 4 years and has now enrolled herself in Rock School of London for her assessments. She is now a budding pianist and a responsible child. We couldn't be prouder of working as a family to instil these rich early years experience during her developmental years.'

—Mr. Jai Ballani, father of Sera.

9. Shifting the lens—Do eminent personalities of today's modern world connect success to their early life experiences?

Early-year experiences and our families/friends are our first playground to develop relationships with parents/siblings/ peers in the management team. All that happens in early years clearly influence how we manage relationships and eventually the person we become.

We tracked industry leaders/ eminent personalities to deep dive into their early years experiences. Here are some parameters on which qualitative research was performed:

- Early Years Experiences
- Schooling & Education
- Role of ECE & Socio Emotional Development
- Role of ECE & Leadership
- Achievements
- Leadership Reflections
- Conclusion

The studies conducted by the author over years, argue that the impact of Etiquette learning to achieve success in life success is positive. It is noticeable that displaying etiquette is characteristic of leadership qualities. It will be fair to remark that a leader's personal history (family influence or early life experience at home/school) and this same environment's responses to key life skills/trigger events play a significant role in shaping emotional intelligence and etiquette learning.

Although success is subjective, the leaders interviewed for this study display similar patterns in their lifestyle to achieve what they have, so far. Some are impacted by their father's etiquettes and core values, while others are impacted by their mother's patience, tolerance and acceptance of diversity.

To be a leader of a thriving organisation, one should display fearlessness, empathy, resilience, to be able to create an example for others, decision making, sustainability, confidence, self-awareness and self-management. One of the key elements, significant to be a leader according to the author, is to spread awareness among educators and caregivers that early years are the best years to nurture social environment, family values, etiquette, social mannerisms.

9.1 Eminent Personality—Soldier Scholar | Conflict Management | Social Transformation

Lt Gen Arjun Ray (Retd) is a man with an experience of a lifetime in war, conflict and peace. Having served in the army for 38 years, he possesses a practical and theoretical insight into combating conflict situations, insurgency, and post-conflict reconstruction. It is a complete honour to have such an eminent personality to be a part of this research on Impact of early years on life success.

Early Years Experience

Born in Calcutta, Lieutenant General Arjun Ray completed his schooling at St Xavier's School, Jaipur, and graduated from the University of Rajasthan with a degree in humanities. He is a graduate of the prestigious British Army Staff College at Camberley, England, the Higher Command Course and the National Defence College. He served as India's Deputy Military Advisor in London from 1986 to 1989.

His early years were greatly dominated by the 1947 Hindu-Muslim riots. He recalls being a midnight child motivated to do something for the country. He speaks to us how etiquette learning and emotional intelligence areas were focused on, and hence, developed in early years such as taking care of oneself, self- awareness, time management, creativity, independence, critical thinking, mindfulness, public speaking, self-management and coping with emotions.

Schooling and Education

Till the age of five (till 1950), I was studying in pre-primary schools in Khetri, a copper mining town. I do not remember the names of nursery schools.

My formal schooling was in St Xavier School, Jaipur (Rajasthan) where I graduated from Senior Cambridge in 1958. They would have my records (hopefully).

After School, I joined Rajasthan College, Jaipur, in 1959 and graduated in 1962. Thereafter, I was commissioned into the Army on 9th February, 1964.

I completed my M.Sc. Defence Studies from the University of Madras in 1990.

Role of ECE and Socio Emotional Development

The restrictive communication atmosphere during early years in turn taught him to manage himself and become empowered and self-reliant. Growing up with an English mother made him a very secular and global-centric individual who made conscious efforts to be a successful leader. However, realisation of an important quality of empathy dawned upon him only when he successfully launched Operation Sadbhavna to win over alienated communities into the mainstream, and bring peace to Ladakh. It is only then that he realised how empathetic and compassionate he was. This was a crucible experience that he recollected at the age of 55 and related back to his early years.

Role of ECE and Leadership

The following years mentioned were the most important early years experiences that according to Lieutenant General Arjun Ray shaped his leadership

1. **Independent thinking:** His parents never interfered with his choices of which school, or university, he should study in; or which career he should pursue.
2. **Self-directed learner:** No tuition, no extra classes. No homework supervision.
3. **Secular and open-minded:** He owes this to his English mother, who was respectful of all religions and Indian customs and rituals.
4. **Acceptance of diversity:** His circle of friends came from diverse backgrounds—religion, economic background, and social status. He grew up in an environment of cognitive diversity.

His one advice to budding leaders would be to be self-aware, know oneself and to have a vision. His mantra is 'Greater energy and greater passion is more extraordinary than greater genius.' His future vision, as he says is that he plans to introduce virtual and augmented reality and nano-teaching pedagogies in a big way in all the schools he is associated with. He says, 'We will also provide every encouragement and opportunity for our students, and teachers, to aspire to become self-driven, ambitious entrepreneurs keen to launch their own start-ups.'

Achievements

A soldier-scholar of the Indian Army, Lt General Arjun Ray, PVSM, VSM (Retd.), has wide-ranging experience in matters of defence and conflict management. But he also has a deep-rooted passion for social transformation. He is the CEO/MD of the Indus Trust and provides vision and strategic direction to all Indus International Schools and Institutions. IB World has recently acknowledged General Ray as one of the six IB World School Leaders for rethinking education and making a high-quality education affordable to the underprivileged.

An alumnus of the globally renowned Staff College, Camberley, UK and former military advisor to the Indian High Commission, UK, during his 38 years of service in the highly-disciplined and 1.2 million-strong Indian Army, Gen Arjun Ray rose to the apex position of the military corps. In his last assignment before his voluntary retirement in 2002, as commander of the 14th Corps in Ladakh on the Indo-China border, he played the lead role in befriending and integrating alienated citizens in the border areas into the

national mainstream by conceptualising and implementing Operation Sadbhavana (goodwill). Under this programme, he set up 13 schools, 11 women's'™ empowerment and 60 adult education centres along the Line of Control in Jammu and Kashmir. In recognition of this service in nation-building, Gen Ray was awarded the Param Vishisht Seva Medal, the highest award of the armed forces for distinguished service in 2002.

Conclusion

Some highlights from the research of Lt General Ray's life journey has strong traces of positive and independent experiences as a child which turned him into a fearless and optimistic leader. He seems to have developed great confidence and greater self-esteem due to the influence of his parents.

As an avid reader since childhood, his early interests were subjects such as political science and history. The three best qualities he developed during his growing years were: Habit of reading, to think critically and to look at the bigger picture. For him in early years being independent meant having a point of view and Freedom to follow his dreams. His parents who belonged to the pre-Baby Boomer Age believed in letting children develop on their own. His mother insisted on punctuality, good manners, socialisation and dressing according to the circumstance. This developed values of independence in him and he turned out to be a risk-taker.

Today, Lt Gen Ray firmly believes that to achieve excellence one must imbalance oneself first; and then regain balance and then have strategies to maintain balance. His team members believe that Lt Gen Arjun is a person who leads by example. A person who has a vision. A person who can manage chaos and uncertainty. He defines himself as a visionary leader and success to him means 'Creating more leaders than followers. Failure is the first step in success. Happiness for oneself and others.'

9.2 Eminent Personality—Actor | Director

Dr Ramesh Arvind

Ramesh Aravind is a popular Indian actor, filmmaker, and television presenter, who although mainly works in Kannada and Tamil films, has also worked in a few Telugu, Malayalam and Bollywood films. He is the most recent actor from the industry to get an honorary doctorate. He is a very successful and yet the most humble person, the author had the honour of researching and interviewing.

Early Years Experience

Dr Ramesh believes it was primarily his father, whose positive influences in the early years shaped the success he has tasted in life today. Essential life skills such as patience, empathy, kindness was embedded in him by his mother who again walked the talk in her day to day life. Dr Ramesh fondly recalls that not a single time he witnessed his mom lose her cool or get upset and yet she ran a perfect household and raised amazing children in a small town of Tamil Nadu, India. Dr Ramesh owes his creativity to his mom and efficiency and discipline to his dad.

There was a 'No pressure atmosphere' at home. Absolutely no pressure to join any co-curricular activities or skating class/keyboard etc. There was complete freedom to do what he felt like doing! The dream to be an actor was an out of box decision and completely opposite with tradition of family i.e. joining and managing the family business. However, Dr Ramesh strongly recalls his father's unflinching and unquestioned support gave room for young Ramesh to experiment in the world of cinema.

Schooling and Education

Ramesh received his early years education through home schooling, where his father's integrity, respect and discipline had a significant impact on him. He attended classes 1–3 in a Government School at Thangamapuripattanam, a small district in Tamil Nadu. He received his middle school education from Sri Kumaran children's home at the Tata Silk Farm at Basavangudi and his high school education from the National High School at Basavanagudi, Bangalore. He graduated from the National College at Basavanagudi, and completed his education in engineering at University Visvesvaraya College of Engineering.

Role of ECE and Socio Emotional Development

Small incidents at early years can shape great confidence in a human mind. One such incident that Dr Ramesh recalls as a child is how his father would try to build confidence in him by exposing him to difficult circumstances in order for him to develop problem solving ability. Once when he came back home from school sobbing as some kids at school laughed at him due to his inability to understand English words, his father ensured him that it was just a language and he could learn anything. His father's words comforted him and build confidence in him. Nothing since then has ever felt intimidating or overwhelming.

Role of ECE & Leadership

Dr Ramesh recalls that he was given the most positive environment that any child could ask for. Even today he does not resonate with any negativity and trusts people easily. The same was the environment of home and upbringing during the early years—there was absolutely no use of threat or anger. During his formative years, he was exposed to his parents' display of integrity, discipline, humbleness, positive mindset, mindfulness etc. He recalls, 'Whenever we went to temple, the prayers were for "everyone" and not just the family.'

With over a million followers, Dr Ramesh is a proud father and doting husband. He is grateful to his humble beginnings and untouched negatively by his supreme success. His message to the young generation is the following five key take-aways:

1. You are part of the bargain. Keep your part of the bargain.
2. Always keep learning
3. Choose the path of love.
4. Keep emotional balance. Don't be impulsive.
5. You are only your thoughts.

Achievements

Dr Ramesh Aravind has to his credit over 100 Kannada films in addition to Tamil, Telugu and Hindi films as the protagonist. He wrote the script for 'Hoomale', the national award-winning film in 1998. The film also won Ramesh the Best Actor Filmfare Award and the Karnataka State Award. His script for a hit film called Amrithadhare in 2005 won him the

Raghavendra Chitravani Award for Best Story. Ramesh Aravind's first directorial venture was the successful 'Rama Shama Bhama' with Kamal Haasan. When Kamal Haasan presented him with the offer to direct Uttama Villain, Dr Ramesh Aravind ceased signing any Kannada films and exclusively began preparation for his directorial debut in Tamil films. It was his first film where he was not the protagonist, but directed the film for his mentor K. Balachander.

He is also a motivational speaker and has spoken on various platforms such as TedX. His recent video shot at BHIVE was viewed more than half a million times in twenty-four hours. His second BHIVE video has been viewed more than a million times and received more than 25,000 actions. Ramesh Aravind has won a number of awards as an actor, director and writer.

He was given an honorary doctorate degree by Rani Channamma University for his contribution to the field of cinema. In the year 2022, he was awarded the 'Dr Shivarama Karanth Huttora Prashasti' or the 'Dr Shivarama Karanth Award' This award is presented to him considering his services on a national level as an actor, director and resource person.

Conclusion

One of the significant parallels that can be drawn in this study as well is the fierce independence Dr Ramesh displayed at an early age. Dr Ramesh was responsible for his actions and decisions—from handling the finances to deciding whether to participate in school field trips. This independence led him join the film industry as a young adult. Till today one witnesses his graceful controlled demeanour and confidence in this high pressured film industry which is significantly attributed to his independent thinking and decision making abilities cultivated during his early years.

He firmly believes that he 'struck a lottery' by being born to parents who had a positive approach to life. He attributes his happiness to his parents. The development of important emotional, cognitive, and behavioural skills took place early in his life. His early years were crucial for the development of a secure emotional attachment and the skills that helped him succeed in life. His parents' way of promoting and developing these life skills along with strengthening core values were important for him to have this undying confidence, patience, and empathy.

9.3 Eminent Personality—Lawyer Sajai Singh

Sajai is the Chair of the International Bar Association (IBA) Technology Law Committee. He is an acclaimed compliance lawyer with more than 32 years of experience representing a wide variety of industries, businesses and sectors. He is also the Co-Chair of the JSA's Corporate Practice which is a leading national law firm in India with over 380+ professionals operating out of seven offices.

Early Years Experience

It was an enriching experience to interview Sajai's parent Ms. Krishna Singh, a Rajput Princess from the principality of Baghsuri. She fondly recalls Sajai being this perfect son who has been raised with encouraging traditions of the Rajput culture—trained in a code of conduct based on respect, valour, integrity and honour. One incident that she recalls is that as a young child when taken to a popular toy store, Sajai surprised his mom with extreme mannerism and politely refused an offer to buy any toy that he would like from the shop. Both interviews with parents have provided great insight into many childhood stories of young Sajai, managing himself and studying completely on his own.

It's remarkable to witness how well the household welcomes and treats guests as well as to the domestic help. Not only their wellbeing is taken into consideration, but also their small needs. Sajai like his father ensured the well-being of each of his cadets and household personnel.

Here are some excerpts from Sajai's proud father Lt Gen Ajai Singh(Retd) interview.

> As his Father, let me share some aspects of Sajai's growth and upbringing. We belong to a well-known JHALAS Clan of Rajputs of Rajasthan which is famous for their Bravery and Self-Sacrifice. The most popular personalities of this Clan AJJA and SAJJA displayed their courageous fighting spirit along with Rana Sanga against the Mughal Invasion by Babar. It is during this battle, where both the brothers displayed their Valor and Self-Sacrifice. With that background my visionary father named me Ajai.
>
> It so happened that the day Sajai was born I had to leave for the INDO PAK War of 1965. However, moments before I left, Sajai was born. Looking at him made me realize that he, the baby continuously stared into my eyes. It is at that very moment, I had decided to name him SAJAI. On the battleground

under enemy tank fire, I wrote an inland letter to name our child SAJAI. That letter is still with my wife, Mrs. Krishna. As an army officer in my entire career, I have tried to emulate these qualities of my namesake AJJA with many decorations on war. Sajai has also displayed the same and much more in the 'Battle of Life' at both personal and professional level. And we both derive our inspirations from the most humble, dignified and courageous Lady Krishna!

Schooling & Education:

Sajai began his Nursery schooling at Sophia School, Ajmer. His prep school i.e. kindergarten was with Sangrur Preparatory School, Punjab.

From Grades 1–3, Sajai was enrolled in St Joseph's Convent School, Pathankot. Convent of Jesus & Mary Ambala Cantonment is where he completed his Grades 3–5. Grades 6–8 and 9–12 both were completed in Kendriya Vidyalaya MHOW, Indore & Ambala Cantonment respectively.

He graduated with a Bachelor in Science from St John's College Agra. He further pursued a Management course from Indian Institute of Marketing and Management Delhi and LLB from Delhi University. Finally, an executive course in Negotiation Skills was completed at Wharton, Philadelphia, US.

Role of ECE in Socio Emotional Development

Sajai witnessed his father leading a very disciplined life. However, due to his work, Sajai was required to change places every two years, leaving behind his friends and neighbours.

While children his age were using their early years to forge friendships for life, he was meeting new people and seeking commonalities that would allow him to blend in easily.

His parents through all the change taught him some interesting values to live by. His mom always said, 'Success will come and go, but integrity is forever.' Her words somehow remained through all the ups and downs of his life. Sajai's sister Ms. Shambhavi fondly recalls Sajai's ability to spot opportunities and convert them into something meaningful. Perhaps it has been his greatest strength–which she quotes is an 'intuitive gift that Sajai was born with. Childhood experiences only helped him to recognise that these opportunities were sometimes hidden in adversity.'

In 1983, his father Lt Gen Ajai Singh, was posted in London on an assignment, where he was intrigued by the environment he was exposed to. While the military atmosphere remained similar to the one in India, there were differences that intrigued him. Looking back, he now wonders perhaps these sudden and complete changes in his early years made him ready to adapt to new circumstances. Now he laughingly adds, 'No place is fearful, no person unfriends able. I probably seek change and welcome it wholeheartedly.'

Role of ECE & Leadership

Despite the ups and downs of life, Sajai believes in utmost trust, integrity and respect for all the people he comes across. He learnt that every person who trusts you, will spread the word of that trust to others, who will do the same to others. The value of the trust others had in him went far beyond anything that can be measured. This very trust propelled him to a global level of visibility that he had not anticipated. He got elected to the Executive Committee of ITechLaw in 2010 and was the first Asian to have made it to the Executive Committee.

He is equally passionate about education, and regularly conducts seminars on client education, executive education programs and boot camps for young lawyers. The Cyberspace Camp™ program is one such program he has patronised and promoted in several developing nations. His training sessions are highly rated. One of the participants remarked, 'Sajai came with so much personal insight. It felt like this was an assimilation of years of observation and numerous personal encounters.'

Sajai is the former President of ITechLaw, the International Technology Lawyers Association, headquartered in the US. This is a first for any Asian!

Achievements

From speaking at ITechLaw events, he has moved on to positions of responsibility. He has chaired the Education Committee and revived the Cyberspace Camp program of the erstwhile CLA. He also joined the Board of ITechLaw and took over the reins of ITechLaw's India conference.

He first Asian to make it to the Executive Committee of ITechLaw in 2010 and was the. He is also an acclaimed transactional lawyer representing a wide variety of industries, businesses and sectors funnel investments into India.

This wealth of experience means that he understands the issues that arise in major transactions and can provide solutions to resolve these issues—providing advice that goes well beyond legal and contractual matters, and into the technical and commercial heart of the success of the transaction.

Conclusion

Interactions with Sajai and his parents proves that great leaders are not born but are made over time, by inculcating etiquette learning and rich life experiences in early years. Sajai's magnetic persona walks the talk of all things which are fine and graceful!

He once was asked why we did not light a bulb instead of lighting an oil lamp at the Conference in India, since it would remove darkness as well. His responded bringing forth the spiritual significance of the traditional oil lamp.

> The oil in the lamp symbolises our negative tendencies and the wick, the ego. When lit by knowledge, the negativities get slowly exhausted and the ego too finally perishes. The flame of a lamp always burns upwards. Similarly acquisition of knowledge generally guides the individual towards higher ideals.

His early experiences set him to believe that he can make good of any opportunity. Sajai believes that where one ends up depends a lot on one's attitude and experience, skills and availability of resources.

His Life Mantra is 'Do your duty and leave the rest to the Universe'.

9.4 Eminent Personality—Technology Leader | Investor | Innovator Karishma Lalwani

Karishma is a technology leader, keynote speaker, early start-up investor and a mentor at Salesforce—a top cloud CRM software company. She has over 17 years of work experience across the globe, such as in India, UK and US (where she currently resides) helping enterprises design and build software applications to digitise their business. She is a mother of two young kids, a five-year-old boy and a new-born girl. She believes in the 'servant leadership' philosophy built on the belief that the most effective leaders strive to serve others, rather than accrue power or take control.

Early Years Experience

Karishma grew up in a joint family of 15 people in a 3-bedroom house in Mumbai with her parents, grandparents, uncles, aunts and cousins. During one of the interactions, she revealed that the small and loving village to which she belonged, made her a secure and confident human being in life. Her early years memories are full of laughter, joy, excitement and a place where all her needs were met in a timely and loving manner—a true home. This has been one of the key factors in her will to create lasting bonds in her own work and personal life. She speaks four languages fluently and her mom recalls her being great at conversations from a very early age (even before she started walking). There was a huge emphasis on educating girl children in her family to ensure they grow up to be financially independent women who can overcome any life situation. She is extremely grateful to her parents for sponsoring her education all the way up to graduation.

Schooling & Education

Born and raised in Mumbai, she did her kindergarten and first grade at St. Lawrence school in Santacruz. Thereafter, she spent the rest of her school years at St. Louis Girls convent school where she learnt important life lessons like discipline, time management, value of hard work and perseverance. After school, she pursued her graduation in STEM from Jai Hind college, Mumbai—a premier college to study Science/STEM courses. In 2001, due to her high scores in the 12th final exams she got accepted into the Computer Engineering program at the prestigious Thadomal Shahani Engineering college (Mumbai University) and graduated in 2005 along with a confirmed job offer from one of the largest multinational consulting firms, Accenture technology services.

Role of ECE & Socio Emotional Development

While interviewing her parents, they shared a specific incident with us.

'Karishma overslept in her school bus when she was three years old. She had to find her way back home through the streets of Mumbai. Due to the negligence of her school, she found herself in an empty bus compound and had no adult nearby to guide her back to school or home. However, she summoned up the courage to approach two young homeless boys (10–13 years old) and requested their assistance to walk with her home. Not only was she brave enough to navigate the way and lead the path but also offered them her lunchbox.'

While narrating the story, it was evident that her father still felt nervous to recall this particular incident.

Role of ECE & Leadership

She believes in leading with empathy and authenticity. This very well resonates with the fact that she grew up in a home with people of different ages, genders and roles, which taught her the value of teamwork, empathy, communication skills and conflict resolution. What reflects strongly is her steadiness, be it academics or work. Although she did wither some storms of life, she received constant love and support of her parents and the rest of her family which she fondly calls as her village. Her confidence that was nurtured in early years is very well evident even today with her capability of being a mother and simultaneously growing in her career.

A true believer in leading by example, Karishma says that she never asks her team to work on a task that she wouldn't work on herself. Her technical expertise and hardworking nature have made it possible for her to be promoted to the Senior Director of Product at a young age of thirty-five at Salesforce which is a leading cloud company in the world. Karishma has managed people twice her age due to the depth of knowledge she holds and her leadership abilities. Although it was intimidating to be a young manager at first, she stayed humble and true to her core value of leading by example.

Achievements

She spent four years consulting with Accenture followed by four years in CapGemini and has spent the last decade working on core cloud product teams at Salesforce. She has led over twenty-five digital transformation projects throughout her career including major financial services organisations in the US like Bank of America, JP Morgan Chase, Farmers Insurance as well as Bajaj Finserv and IDFC in India. She has filled our patents focused on innovation in tech and has been a speaker at multiple conferences. She has won numerous awards for her performance and was chosen as the woman of the Monday in June 2021 for her commitment and leadership during the Covid pandemic. The highlight of her career was when she was presented with the opportunity to lead a fireside chat with the cofounder and the president of technology at Salesforce to talk about the latest innovations on the Salesforce platform.

Karishma is a strong advocate for increasing the ratio of women in tech and encourages girls to get educated in

STEM. Personally, she recalls the numerous times when she was the only woman technologist in a conference room with twenty men and constantly had to prove herself to her peers, leaders and sometimes even to her team. She was disheartened to attend an architect conference in San Francisco where she was one out of only five women in a conference of 400 professionals. She knew then, that there a lot has to be done to bring diversity in the field of technology. She firmly believes the only way to do this is to start early (right from first grade) to create gender parity in the field of Science, Technology, Engineering and Mathematics.

Being the only women leader to be featured in this research, Karishma also has been a true trailblazer in her family and professional life by being the first woman to pursue education in engineering, first to get a job offer to work in the UK and US, first five women in the world to attain Salesforce Architect certification and first woman in her father's side of the family to

continue to pursue her career as a mother. She builds conversations with her five-year-old son about making the world a fair place for men and women.

Conclusion

Karishma's exposure to a larger family that taught her valuable lessons in life and has made her a social, spiritual, family oriented professional. Though she is daddy's girl even now, being among an array of cousins and learning the art of sharing, caring and many other etiquettes, till date Karishma has an inherent quality that of a nurturer and a leader.

She hopes to be a role model for young girls to chase their dreams without succumbing to the social pressure of traditional roles of being a homemaker played by many women. She also wants girls to know that with hard work and perseverance it is possible to have a career and kids and excel at both roles in life.

10. The journey continues...!

From the recent case studies of Industry leaders and ongoing studies of the ELPS curriculum, it's safe to conclude that ensuring healthy experiences in their early years and etiquette learning helps young children to understand appropriate, polite and considerate behaviour. This enables them to form positive experiences, good manners and become more socially attentive as they get older. Early years facilitators play a crucial role in imparting social skills to kindergarten children. Polite behaviour and social skills are as important as other academic learning.

Even though the scope of my study currently encompasses

the journey of the most successful elite in their respective fields and to determine how the early years impacted their choice in middle/high school, universities, career, life and parenting, it aims to conduct more studies with more diverse communities. The study therefore, focuses on the need to implement curriculums such as ELPS as a part of the ongoing kindergarten/home-schooling programs. This can enhance a child's social emotional development. Early years educators who have the ability to design kindergarten curriculum now possess the capacity to lay a foundation which can be made strong with the right learning and teaching.

REFERENCES

Young, Mary Eming. *Early Child Development: Investing in the Future*. Washington D. C.: The World Bank, 1996.

Lazorchak, Shirley. "Business Protocol and Etiquette: Preparing Students for the Global Business Environment." *Journal of Family & Computer Sciences* (January 2000). https://www.questia.com/library/journal/1P3-50861472/businessprotocol-and-etiquette-preparing-students

Willis, Clarissa A. and Pam Schiller. "Preschooler's Social Skills Steer Life Success." *Young Children* 66, no. 1 (January 2011): 42–49.

Lazar, Irving, Richard Darlington, Harry Murray, Jacqueline Royce, Ann Snipper, and Craig T. Ramey. "Lasting effects of Early Education: A Report from the Consortium for

Longitudinal Studies." *Monographs of the Society for Research in Child Development* 47, no. 2/3 (1982): i–151. https://doi.org/10.2307/1165938.

Jarrold, William, Peter Mundy, Mary Gwaltney, Jeremy Bailenson, Naomi Hatt, Nancy McIntyre, Kwanguk Kim, Marjorie Solomin, Stephanie Novotny and Lindsay Swain. "Social Attention in a Virtual Public Speaking Task in Higher Functioning Children with Autism." *Autism Res* 6, no. 5 (October 2013): 393–410. https://doi.org/10.1002/aur.1302

Paley, Vivian. "The Uses of Dramatics in Kindergarten." *The University of Chicago Press Journals* 78, no. 5 (1978).

"The importance of Etiquette in a civil society." *Etiquette*. https://www.candacesmithetiquette.com/importance-of-etiquette.html

Mark, T. "How early life experiences shape the leader you become." Mint Lounge. September 5, 2022. https://lifestyle.livemint.com/news/talking-point/how-early-life-experinces-shape-the-leader-you-become-111662348578453.html

Ballani, Simran. "Etiquette Learning and Public Speaking: Early Etiquette Learning and Its Impact on Higher Education and Working Professionals." *International Journal of Educational and Pedagogical Sciences* 14, no. 7 (2020). https://publications.waset.org/10011315/etiquette-learning-and-public-speaking-early-etiquette-learning-and-its-impact-on-higher-education-and-working-professional

Bakken, Linda, Nola Brown and Barry Downing. "Early Childhood Education: The Long-Term Benefits.' *Journal of Research in Childhood Education* 31, no. 2 (2017): 255–269. doi:10.1080/02568543.2016.1273285

DR SUE ALLINGHAM
Independent Consultant, Author and Trainer, UK

Dr. Sue gained an MA and then a Doctorate—both in Early Childhood Education, from Sheffield University. This led to her becoming a Local Authority Early Years Adviser, enabling her to develop her practice working with provision across the EYFS. She has written two books that support practice across the Early Years and into Key Stage One – *Transitions in the Early Years* and *Emotional Literacy in the Early Years.*

DR KATHRYN MURRAY
Founder of Future Strong Education Consultancy, Australia.

Dr. Kathy is a Classroom Design expert using her original Brain-SET Formula© for Classroom Design research. Kathryn works globally and uses her 40 years of experience, research and intuition to support children, educators, teachers, leaders, and parents to be the best they can be.

EIGHT

RELATIONSHIPS AND COMMUNICATION IN SUPPORTING CHILDREN'S BEHAVIOUR

Part1: 'We aren't little people, we're children'

In June 1993 Loris Malaguzzi gave a lecture in which he said:

> There are hundreds of different images of the child. Each one of you has inside yourself an image of the child that directs you as you begin to relate to a child. This theory within you pushes you to behave in certain ways; it orients you as you talk to the child, listen to the child, observe the child. It is very difficult for you to act contrary to this internal image. For example, if your image is that boys and girls are very different from one another, you will behave differently in your interactions with each of them.
>
> (These comments are translated and adapted from a seminar presented by Professor Loris Malaguzzi in Reggio Emilia, Italy, June 1993)

AS WE are in the middle of a global pandemic, we believe it is time we took a step back and reflect on practices and provisions for the youngest children in our settings. The last two years have made a severe impact on us all. The world has changed. Our surroundings have changed. As adults we have had years of life experiences, from which we can draw upon to help us to work things through. Children however, have not had this. Therefore, as the more experienced adults, it has naturally come to us to support the children through this time of change, or 'transition'.

A transition is a process and not an event, and we all deal with these in different ways. To cope with any transition, requires us to communicate our feelings in a variety of ways. We all have different ways of expressing ourselves physically and emotionally. These are deeply rooted in our traditions, culture, upbringing, lifestyle and experiences. As teachers of young children, we are obliged to address who we are and how we manifest ourselves as this will be a lens through which we view the children and families. This is the point that Malaguzzi is making above. He goes on to say:

> The environment you construct around you and the children also reflects this image you have about the child. There's a difference between the environment that you are able to build based on a preconceived image of the child and the environment that you can build that is based on the child you see in front of you—the relationship you build with the child, the games you play. An environment that grows out of your relationship with the child is unique and fluid.

> The quality and quantity of relationships among you as adults and teachers also reflects your image of the child. Children are very sensitive and can see and sense very quickly the spirit of what is going on among the adults in their world. (ibid)

One way that children will manifest their thinking, feelings and emotions will be through how they behave. They may not have the language to articulate their feelings thus, their behaviour becomes a way of communicating needs.

With this in mind, reflect on this case study considering these three statements:

- Communication through behaviour
- Self-regulation and social and emotional skills
- 'We aren't little people, we're children'

> Child A was interesting right from the minute the teachers did their home visit. He lived in a small modern house that was immaculate and, unless you knew otherwise, you would never have known that three children lived there as there were no toys or other thing lyging around. 'A' wanted his visitors to see his room, which he shared with his elder brother. It contained only beds, a large television and several toy cars, which 'A' had lined up neatly along the edge of the rug. 'A's' older brother and sister already had attended the school and were known by the visiting teachers He also had a baby brother who was in his mother's arms throughout the visit.
>
> In this environment 'A' appeared to be calm and well

behaved. When he started at school, things were very different. He could not control himself, wouldn't listen and was very disruptive. The only person he would respond to positively in any way was his older sister. 'A' also had not been to any type of pre-school. Child 'B' started in the same class as 'A' at the same time. His mother did not want a home visit and this decision was respected by the practitioners. The family were refugees and there was no father or fatherly figure present. At school, 'B' showed very similar behaviour to 'A' and, although they competed with each other, it was often the two of them against the world, as other children did not like their activities destroyed.

They were able to play alongside, but not with, each other. Child 'B' had also not been to a pre-school. With both of these boys in the same room clear plans needed to be made to minimise disruption. Small circle times were introduced using puppets to encourage talking and turn taking. Hand signals and pictures were used to gain attention meaningfully demonstrating purpose.

Positive reinforcement was used instead of reprimands. The adults developed games to be played in small groups to promote taking turns and celebrate success. The day child 'A' and child 'B' were noted playing outside with the train together for a concentrated period was a breakthrough (adapted from my book *Transitions in the Early Years,* Published by Practical Pre-School Books 2011).

- What were the boys communicating?
- How were they doing it?
- What did the adults do?

So much of what happened for these two boys could have been deemed as 'bad behaviour' and subsequently punished. They were young children, with English as an additional language finding their way in a new environment and expressing themselves. Fortunately, in such circumstances, the adults understood the children's position and worked with it.

As adults it is all too easy for us to make assumptions about the children we work with and their behaviour. But we must keep in mind what a little boy once said to me 'We aren't little people, we're children'. It is wrong of us to expect children to behave like mini adults.

- Think about a situation, or group, where you feel comfortable.
- Why do you feel like that?
- How do you know?

Conversely, think of situations or places where you feel uncomfortable and consider why this is so.

- If you don't have to, do you revisit these situations?
- And if you do, what are your coping strategies?

Remember that children do not choose to go to school and keep returning to it every day. It is brought upon them, which is a drastic change in their lives.

> Child 'F' was a little boy who loved motorbikes. When the teachers visited him at his house, he was in the garden riding round on his motorbike wearing his own set of leathers while his dad was working on a bike nearby. He excitedly showed his little bike to his visitors and they were very impressed with his knowledge. When 'F' started in the reception class, it became clear that his interests lay in constructing and creating.
>
> The teachers were happy to feed this interest and develop it with relevant magazines and pictures. Child 'F' had not been to pre-school (adapted from my book *Transitions in the Early Years.* Published by Practical Pre-School Books 2011).

Helping children to adapt and settle is about supporting them to self-regulate. To understand that their emotions are relevant and important and similar to those of the adults'. But this is not possible unless we take time to demonstrate our own self-regulation and supportive co-regulation to help children feel comfortable, be known and settle into their settings. This means understanding the key principle that every child is unique.

> Self-regulation depends on and grows out of co-regulation, where adults and children work together towards a common purpose, including finding ways to resolve conflicts in any domain, and returning to a well-balanced state of mind and health. Over time and with consistent practice, the process shifts from

> co-regulation between adult and child to the child's self-regulation. The flexibility of brain cells and pathways in the early years means that the brain's architecture is altered in response to the quality and consistency of co-regulation experiences, building the capacity for self-regulation. In its earliest stages, co-regulation involves a carer helping a baby who is overwhelmed by feelings, perhaps from being hungry, uncomfortable, or unhappy for any reason to return to a state of calm. Through voice, sensitive handling, and tuning in to respond promptly to a baby's signals, the adult helps the baby experience returning to balance after being in a state of emotional arousal. Each experience of co-regulation helps to build the neural pathways that regulate emotion.

However, this takes some time, and initial transitions can be difficult to start with if the team does not consider the wellbeing of the children involved and how this period of transition would affect them. How different would this have been if any of the children outlined above had been shouted at, made to sit on a 'naughty chair', had their names put on the 'rain cloud' of the 'behaviour chart', been kept inside when they wanted to be outside, sent to the headteacher, or forced to do inappropriate activities. The list is endless but the negative results are easy to guess. Sadly, all too often children are talked down to, ordered to do things or their feelings are completely ignored or dismissed at home and in their settings. Unfortunately, as some of the boys from the above examples progressed through the school system, they became disaffected as their wellbeing was increasingly disregarded. This resulted in two of them being excluded.

This reflection on the emotional environment must include the feelings of the adults as well. We can probably all remember a time of transition at some point in our lives that may or may not have gone very well. Reflecting on our own experiences and how we felt about them will enable us to better understand the children.

Remember 'We aren't little people, we are children.' This was once said to me by a five-year-old boy when I referred to him and his classmates as 'little people'. It was a real penny drop moment for me and I admired him for speaking out. He wasn't being cheeky or rude, but was just stating the facts. It was clear that the environment and adults around him were supportive of him, making him aware of himself and his agency.

It is important to make clear from the outset that to feel positive socially and emotionally, and to know that you are cared about, understood and respected is crucial for all humans throughout their lives.

Feelings and emotions are triggered by many things and can either be positive or negative. We do not react in the same way to the same things. For example, some children are scared of balloons, clowns or some fairy stories whilst others love them. Just in the same way as some adults can be triggered by certain smells or sounds that others enjoy. It is our responsibility to be proactive, to be noticing and listening adults. Children cannot always tell us that something makes them uncomfortable. Not all children have been enabled to express themselves in the way the little boy in the example above did.

In order to be proactive in nurturing self-regulation and social and emotional skills, it is crucial that the children are not seen as 'little people', but as children with rights and agency. This means that the environment in which we work with them must be co-constructed with them. We must not make assumptions about what they might like, want or need.

In this way we must consider not just the physical environment that we provide, but also the emotional environment.

How do we facilitate this growth in practical terms in the environment?

Malaguzzi states that we must respond to the real child who presents to us, rather than a preconceived idea and reflect this in the environments we live in.

In order to do this, we have to reflect and differentiate on the purpose of the rules we create—if they are helpful to the children, or do they exist to make life easier for the adults.

How often have we reflected on how the sessions work in our settings?

How does this next case study make you feel?

> It was the first time that the little boy had been left at the setting. He had previously visited with his mother, but she had left him there this time. The family did not speak English and had not been in the area for very long. He was three years old.
> He would not take his coat off which was buttoned right up to his neck. It was about 10:30 am meaning that he had been at the preschool for an hour and a

> half. All the while, he had been wandering around quietly whimpering and talking to himself. A visitor had just arrived to do some observations, which upset him, as he had thought it was his mother coming back. The visitor enquired as to which member of the team was his Key Person. An adult was indicated. She was sitting at a table with her back to the child, working with a group. As the visitor watched, the little boy continued to wander as his Key Person finished with her group and started to set the table for snack time. No one was interacting with the little boy.
>
> Children were called over for snacks and the Key Person sat with them. All the chairs around the table were filled.
>
> Suddenly the little boy noticed where his Key Person was. He stopped whimpering, found a spare chair and dragged it over to be next to her. She turned, saw him and asked him not to put his chair next to her, since, there was no room, although some space could easily have been made. He pulled the chair back to where he had found it and started whimpering again (Adapted from Allingham, S., 2020).

Imagine that you were that little boy, being left in a space on your own for the first time with no one who could understand you. What impact would it have on your emotional wellbeing? As a professional how would you cope? Have would you manage to stop this impact affecting your work? What do you need to focus on? These words may help your thinking:

- Expectations
- Personal feelings
- Assumptions
- Outside influences
- Other people

The little boy in the case study needed his adults to consider everything that was impacting on him. He did not understand the environment and the routines were all about the adults.

Use these questions to consider how you support children to develop their social and emotional skills:

The Emotional Environment

- How does my daily routine make it possible for me to get to know and treat each child as an individual?
- How does my environment demonstrate to children that they are welcome?
- How well have new children come to terms with their feelings on admission? How do I know?
- Do we have a partnership with parents that is truly two ways?
- How do the staff interact with each other?
- Do your staff make time to talk with parents and carers. Do the children see their parents sharing friendly conversation and laughter with their practitioners?
- Are the children happy when they arrive? What do they feel when they leave?
- What have I done today (this week) to help the

children to be more aware of their feelings?

- Do we respect the feelings of the children?
- Do we respect the feelings of the families?
- How do my feelings affect how I interact with individuals?
- How do I interact with children? Do I get down at their level and give them a chance to express themselves?
- Are the skills of conversation modelled?
- Do children lead interactions?
- Is open-ended questioning used?
- Are children engaged in their play? Can they approach an adult for support when necessary?
- Does planning reflect the needs of the children?
- How are the children able to be independent to make decisions and choices?
- How does the environment encourage this?
  - Are the resources of good quality and do children value them?
  - Does the routine allow children time to follow through their ideas?
  - Are the children involved in how the environment is set out?
  - What can be seen that is initiated by a child?
  - How does my room arrangement encourage children to talk together, share and co-operate?
  - Is children's own work proudly displayed, or has it been adapted by the adults to 'neaten' it up?
  - Are the displays at a height where the children can see them and become engaged with them?

- Is there only work by the adults on display? Why is this?
- Is everything clean and well cared for?
- How out of date are the displays? Does anyone notice them anymore?

Adapted from Allingham, S. (2020)

Wellbeing

As the responsible adults in the environment, we must be sure that we model and project a feeling of wellbeing.

Ferre Laevers has described the child with a high level of wellbeing as one who feels 'like a fish in water'. In other words, the child is comfortable in their own skin, and more often than not confident in how they are with others. Physically and emotionally, their bodies and minds are balanced. Later in this chapter, we will look at the Leuven scales of wellbeing and involvement and how using these in an informed way will help teachers to have a better understanding of the children they work with.

Using the Leuven Scales of Wellbeing and Involvement

The role of all the adults is to foster an emotionally secure environment where adults and children feel like, to use Professor Laevers term, 'fish in water'. There are two viewpoints to an emotionally secure environment, that of the adult, and that of the children.

Whenever Professor Laevers writes using the word 'children' it is a useful substitute for the word 'adult' so that we can reflect on ourselves and those around us.

> To know how children do in a particular setting, we should explore the degree in which children do feel at ease, act spontaneously, show vitality and self-confidence. All this indicates that their emotional well-being is good. and that their physical needs, the need for tenderness and affection, the need for safety and clarity, the need for social recognition, the need to feel competent and the need for meaning in life and moral value are satisfied.
>
> The second criterion, involvement, is linked to the developmental process and urges the adult to set up a challenging environment favouring concentrated, intrinsically motivated activity.
>
> Care settings and schools have to succeed on both tasks. Only paying attention to emotional well-being and a positive climate is not enough. Efforts to enhance involvement will only have an impact if children and students feel at home and are free from emotional constraints.
>
> Center for Experiential Education – February 2015

Through his work at Leuven University, Professor Laevers noticed that, however effective the teaching, the quality of learning would not be good if the child was emotionally uncomfortable.

He developed what he called the Process Oriented Monitoring System (POMS).

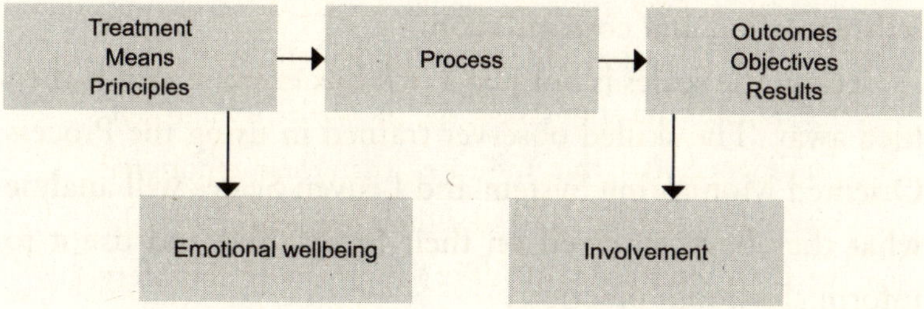

The first box 'treatment, means, principles' means that we must reflect on our provision. What do we demonstrate through our vision, provision and practice? The second box asks us to reflect on the routines, processes and procedures in our settings. Are they appropriate? Do they help us achieve the best possible outcome for children? If not, we must reflect on the process.

None of our outcomes will be as good as they could be if the top line of POMS is not underpinned by the crucial elements of wellbeing and involvement.

In order to better understand children, Professor Laevers developed the Leuven Scales of Wellbeing and Involvement. There are levels in each of the two scales. In each Level One is 'Extremely Low' and Level Five is 'Extremely High'. Each level has a definition to enable the observer to reflect on what they have seen. Using these scales enables teachers to interrogate their observations of a particular child or group of children.

The Leuven Scales are an important tool to help us to understand the children we work with and the impact we, and the environment we set up, have on them. Because wellbeing and involvement are a two-way, reciprocal processes. They are about interactions, emotional security and behaviours, self-regulation and co-regulation.

Using the scales is not just a tick box exercise that is then filed away. The skilled observer trained in using the Process Oriented Monitoring System and Leuven Scales will analyse what they have observed on their focus child and use it to inform classroom practices.

Part 2: 'No one understands me!'

Wellbeing and Social and Emotional Growth in the Classroom

Social and emotional growth happens easily for children if they know that they are safe and feel secure in their relationship with a trusted, stable adult—their key person. Attachment between baby/child and parent and the reciprocal bonding between the adult and the child builds strength and stability within a relationship. All of us thrive when our social and emotional needs are taken care of, and this contributes to our mental and physical wellbeing. As teachers, there are many factors to take into consideration when we acknowledge the needs of children. Think about the children mentioned earlier in this chapter and their need for reassurance and understanding. If each of those children had been attached to someone in the centre, their days would be much smoother.

Attachment and Positive Growth

John Bowlby and Mary Ainsworth described the vital need for a child to be attached to an adult as a method of survival. A baby human cannot survive without the care and protection of an adult human. In order to survive, it is imperative for the baby to be attached and the parent to bond with the baby. Attachment occurs when children have a stable adult they trust, in an environment that is safe and secure. This is called 'secure attachment' and underpins a good grounding for future, trusting relationships (girlfriends, boyfriends, friends, husbands, wives).

There are three other types of attachment styles that result in varying degrees of dependence, poor behaviour, fear of adults, and inability to express or control emotions. These are ambivalent-insecure, avoidant-insecure and disorganised-insecure styles. The impact of these three styles is demonstrated through behaviours that make it difficult to develop relationships and indicates that the child does not feel safe and secure. This influences the child's friendships and relationships and their overall social and emotional development. Providing a consistent, stable caregiver at home or in the classroom is important for every child to enable them to flourish holistically. Relationships developed in the home or classroom environment are linked to the four main attachment styles that are generally and initially formed between parent and child.

At home

Attachment to a parent, grandparent, aunt, uncle in the home environment usually happens naturally. Parents bring home the new baby and everyone wants to cuddle, talk, make faces at and love the new addition to the family. The person who cares for the baby the most (often the mother) becomes the primary carer and is the person the baby becomes attached to the most securely. When the baby is around 6–9 months of age, it cries if any other adult holds it other than the primary carer. This is secure attachment style, and is a normal developmental process.

In some cases, secure attachment to a primary carer does not occur within the premises of a house. This could be due to post-natal depression, working long hours, health issues (mental or physical) or other family disturbances. In this instance, it is very important that the child has another adult to get attached to in the home or family. This makes attachment in an early learning centre extra important too.

The classroom

Generally, there are at least two adults in each classroom in an early learning centre. This provides opportunities for secure attachment for each child to one of the adults. Experiencing a particular attachment style when a child is young has consequences in the classroom and in life.

Each attachment style (secure, avoidant, ambivalent, or disorganised) comes with its own set of behaviours that we may see in the classroom. The degree of attachment or non-attachment affects how children see themselves, interact with others and build relationships. Strong and secure attachment to at least one primary carer in childhood helps children to feel secure, safe, worthy and valued. Children are more inclined to take risks in their learning and develop strong and healthy relationships that they can replicate in adulthood.

Avoidant, ambivalent or disorganised attachment with a primary carer in childhood results in poor self-esteem, lack of self-confidence or self-love, difficulty forming relationships, and managing emotions in varying degrees. Consequently, if a child comes to our classroom displaying non-attachment, then it is our job to provide the opportunity for them to form a secure attachment with us. Our classroom environments should be safe havens so that children can be relaxed and have an emotional connection with the space and the adults.

This means that in the classroom, teachers must consciously make sure that each child has an adult with whom they can develop attachment. Generally, this happens naturally but there are always some children who are harder to connect with or may be very quiet and are overlooked. Think about the children in your class. If there are two or three teachers, each one must have specific children allocated to them to provide an opportunity to form relationships and connections. This must be a conscious decision so that all children are included.

The Brain-SET Formula for Classroom Design developed by Dr Kathryn Murray can help with this. The intentional design of learning spaces in a classroom are planned and curated to consider the development of the brain and facilitate relationships between children and adults. The way we set up the rooms makes a difference to the level of safety experienced by the children and the relationships that develops (Duncan and Murray, 2021; Murray, 2021).

The Brain-SET Formula is about building relationships with every single child in your classroom through authentic, meaningful and purposeful interactions in smaller, well-designed spaces. Having smaller, defined spaces in the classroom means that children are more focused, less threatened, communicate more, and can manage their emotions more effectively.

Strong relationships stir our emotions. The stronger the emotion, the more specific is the memory and the learning that goes along with it. If we can establish a strong connection between us, the children and the parents in memorable ways, we can support children's learning.

To do this we need to be curious about what the children are interested in, what they do on weekends, what food they like. Think about the children you know! Do you know what interests them? In his book, Brain Rules, John Medina reminds us that children are born as natural explorers. In the classroom and using the Brain-SET Formula, we would curate small spaces in a purposeful and intentional way that allows exploration of materials related to children's interests.

Each of the multiple spaces in the classroom are calm and joyful. This helps with e-social and emotional connections, relationships and wellbeing.

The Connection Between Tennis and Communication

Modelling relationship building skills to children supports the development of confidence and allows them to experience security and feel safe and happy. This is done by actively listening to children through a serve and return conversation. Just like a tennis match, the ball (the message we are sending) must go back and fro to each person on opposite sides of the net—serve and return. However, sometimes the tennis net is a barrier to the ball moving from one person to the other. Barriers in communication prevent the message from being heard. It could be that the words used aren't familiar, or English is an additional language, it could be noisy, one person could have a hearing impairment.

Whatever is the reason for the barrier teachers must model and undertake effective communication strategies. In this way, relationships can develop and children will feel heard, acknowledged, valued, and enjoy a sense of belonging.

This means that we should:

- Make eye contact while the child is speaking
- Patiently listen to what the child is saying verbally and non-verbally
- Ask open ended questions to facilitate a discussion about the child's interests

By asking open ended questions like 'I wonder what you would buy if you went shopping and could have anything' and listening to their answer, gives children the respect and opportunity to be heard and valued. We learn a lot just by listening to children. We learn how they think and what excites and interests them. This informs our planning and learning experiences.

Many times, as adults, we half ask a question, and we half listen to the answer. It's our job to teach children how to be respectful of one another and actively listen and respond in a conversation—serve and return.

Maybe you'd like to try this with someone you know. In a pair, person 'A' talks about their day and the person 'B' keeps interrupting or looks distracted. Swap roles.

How did it feel? Did you want to keep talking? Did you feel heard? Was there active listening? Next time you are out having a cup of coffee with a friend, try having a cappuccino conversation. This is where one person's coffee is being drunk hot and the other's cup is still full. One person is listening while the other talks.

By modelling a serve and return conversation we are teaching children patience, self-regulation. We also teach them to work together when they are collaborating in the defined spaces that we design within the classroom.

We all have needs and connections:

In 1943, Abraham Maslow developed Maslow's Hierarchy of Needs. He established five levels of needs experienced by humans. This was revised in 1970 and three more levels were introduced, moving Maslow's Hierarchy of Needs from 5–8 levels.

Let's look at the eight levels of motivation.

MASLOW'S MOTIVATION MODEL

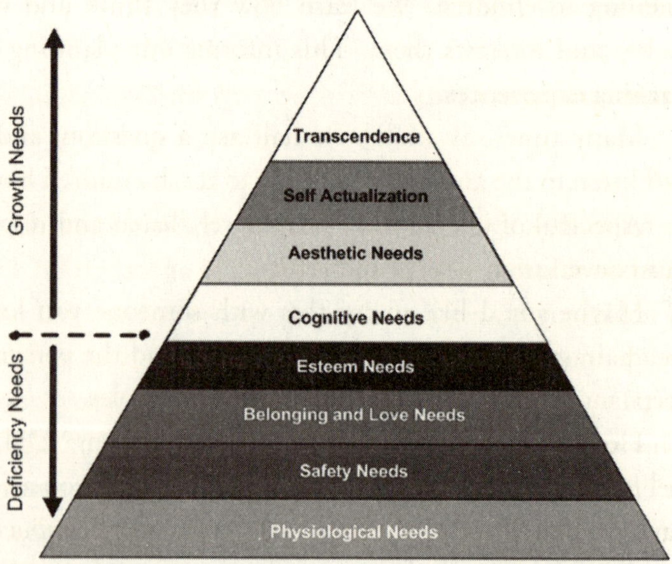

(James Kelly, 2014. https://thepeakperformancecenter.com/educational-learning/learning/principles-of-learning/maslows-hierarchy-needs/)

We begin from the base of the triangle with the most basic of needs.

Physiological needs	– air, water, shelter, warmth, sleep
Safety needs	– security, rules, order, structure
Belonging and love needs	– social needs, affection, family, intimacy
Esteem needs	– self-esteem, self-confidence, achievement, respect
Cognitive needs	–a need to know and understand, knowledge
Aesthetic needs	– appreciation of beauty, balance, self-expression in creative way
Self-Actualisation needs	– realising your own potential, personal growth
Transcendence needs	– helping others to realise their potential

Although everyone has different experiences in life, they must be able to experience some pleasure and a certain degree of achievement, as they move across the triangle. Although we do not expect to be fully satisfied, we can develop a certain amount of satisfaction, as we move forward in life. This can be facilitated through sensitivity in the classroom or environment inside the household that ensures that these basic needs are met. For example, if children do not feel safe. it will be unlikely that they will have high self-esteem or feel self-confident. Using the Brain-SET Formula, classrooms can be environments where Maslow's needs are met in an intentional and purposeful way reflected in each of the carefully designed spaces.

Needs and Behaviour

Understanding needs and how to manage the behaviours having unfulfilled needs met can cause frustration, disappointment, annoyance, or exhaustion. Whatever the feeling, it is quite normal. All parents and teachers feel that way at some point even if they say that they don't. One thing that's important here is that you don't compare yourself to other parents or teachers.

We each have our own 'virtual backpack' that we carry through life. That is, we all have individual skills, beliefs, morals, values, experiences, religion, culture, hopes, dreams, insecurities, likes, and dislikes. Our children are no different. We all carry our own 'backpack' that makes us who we are. But sometimes what's in those backpacks spill out and become poor behaviour choices.

So, what do you do when you have a mutiny in your classroom or house? At home you're running late, the children won't get in the car, lunch boxes aren't packed and you're late for your appointment or work?

Next time you feel emotions rising because of children's behaviour, try these easy steps.

1. **Stop and take a breath**: Actually, stop for 18 seconds and take 3 x 3 seconds deep breaths. Count for three on the way in and three on the way out. In this way oxygen enters your brain and helps with blood circulation. This helps you concentrate more

and think clearly.

2. **Work out the need**: What need isn't being met for your child at that time. Perhaps it's hunger, being overtired, not feeling confident or not feeling safe. Other than that, children (and adults) have two main motivators for their behaviour which are attention and power. There are two others, revenge and avoidance, but they are generally part of the attention and power needs.
3. **Respond to the need you've identified – Attention:** Do they want attention? Give them a hug, or a little job so that they have a responsibility to carry out while you're busy. Connecting with your child fulfils the need for attention in a positive way. You'll know that the need is attention if you feel annoyed.
4. **Respond to the need – Power:** Do they want power? Give them a choice. 'Do you want to get in the car first or last? It's your choice.' Make sure the choice is a win-win outcome. The goal is to get in the car—it doesn't matter if it's first or last. Your child gets to choose and have the power. Their need is fulfilled. If the need is power, you will feel threatened or intimidated.

Each child in the family or classroom is an individual and are of a different age (even six months can make a difference to development). Hence, we can't treat them in exactly the same way. It's important to remember that children are not born bad. They sometimes choose bad behaviours to get what they want and try to fulfil a need or a desire.

Once we start to look at why children are behaving the way they are, we can work out the solution. So, the next time you feel frustrated, remember we all have needs—even we adults—so take a breath, be calm and respond, not react.

Conclusion

As we consider the social and emotional development of children and the impact on wellbeing and self-management of behaviours, some key points are essential to discuss.

It's clear that strengthening relationships with children through attachment to a key person provides a secure basis for future relationships. Using Leuven Scales helps to guide our thinking, planning and shape our classroom practices with the goal of supporting the social and emotional development of all children.

Recognising that we all have needs that motivate our behaviours is key to building relationships that incorporate 'serve and return' conversations using open ended questions—questions asked and responses listened to allow the child to feel heard and the adult to learn much more about the child as a person, not just a student in the classroom.

Ensuring that the classroom environment is aligned with harmonious brain development ensures that children and adults are calmer and enjoy playful interactions that support learning and development. Keeping in mind that 'a calm brain is a thinking brain' (Murray, 2021) when we consider ways to manage behaviours is a valuable reminder to build strong relationships and open communication.

REFERENCES

Allingham, S. *Emotional Literacy in the Early Years: Helping Children Balance Body and Mind.* Practical Pre-School Book, 2020.

Allingham, S. *Transitions in the Early Years.* Practical Pre-School Books, 2011.

Duncan, S. and K. Murray. "A calm brain is a thinking brain: Brain-SET learning environments for young children." *Exchange Press,* 2021. http://exchangepress.com/article/a-calm-brain-is-a-thinking-brain-brain-set-learning-environments-for-young-children/5026142

Kelly, J. "Maslow's Hierarchy of Needs." 2014. https://thepeakperformancecenter.com/educational-learning/learning/principles0of-learning/maslows-hierarchy-needs/

Kendra, C. "What is attachment theory?" verywell mind, 2022. https://www.verywellmind.com/what-is-attachment-theory-2795337.

Laevers, F. *Deep-level-learning and the Experiential Approach in Early Childhood and Primary Education.* Katholieke Universiteit Leuven Research Centre for Early Childhood and Primary Education, 2005.

Medina, J. *Brain Rules (Updated and Expanded): 12 Principles for Surviving and Thriving at Work, Home.* USA: Pear Press, 2014.

Murray, K. "The Brain-SET Formula for classroom design." *The Space,* Spring Edition, 2021.

"Birthe To % Matters: Non Statutory Guidance for the Early Years Foundation Stage." Wordpress, https://birthto5matters.org.uk/

CHARLOTTE HANNAH
Teacher in Wales, UK

Charlotte helps to roll out the new Welsh Curriculum which focuses on child well-being. She has a deep interest in psychology and the relationship between the adult and an inner child. She finds it fascinating that the past remains a prevalent part of our present. Human brains are humanity's greatest asset and also our greatest weakness. Therefore, finding peace in a chaotic world is a Superpower and she helps to find that inner peace.

NINE

CONSCIOUS PARENTING

Do not ask your children to strive

William Martin

Do not ask your children
to strive for extraordinary lives
Such striving may seem admirable,
but it is the way of foolishness.
Help them instead find the wonder
and the marvel of an ordinary life.
Show them the joy of tasting
tomatoes, apples, and pears.
Show them how to cry
when pets and people die.
Show them the infinite pleasure
in the touch of a hand.
And make the ordinary come alive for them.
The extraordinary will take care of itself.

WILLIAM MARTIN'S poem is a beautiful illustration of conscious parenting. He discusses the beauty of teaching the wonders of the world to your child – focusing on their experiences and making 'the ordinary come alive for them.' Such a gentle expression is reminiscent of the encompassing nature of conscious parenting, which aims to reduce the idea that 'discipline' in fact, is the cornerstone to achieving the notion of a golden child.[1] Additionally, conscious parenting accepts that there is no such thing as a 'golden' child. Every child is unique in their own way. Likewise, every child is different and therefore, there is a need to be intuitive and resourceful while raising children. Conscious parenting is the cornerstone of this. Moreover, one of the most important aspects of becoming a conscious parent is becoming conscious of your own inner world. Dr Shefali Tsabary states that we are a human being before we are a parent. Parenting resurrects old feelings and emotions and therefore is an emotionally overwhelming time for them. By becoming aware of this and providing yourself with the necessary tools to regulate and soothe yourself, you are able to meet your child in a calmer, more respondent manner.

This chapter will explore the two components essential to become a conscious parent. Part one will highlight the presence of your inner child and the importance of healing your past. Exploring teachings in Eastern Philosophy, it aims to bring an awareness of how our behaviour is linked to those of our ancestors' through DNA structuring. It will also explore

---

1 Tsabary, Dr Shefali. "The Conscious Parent" Audible, 2015.

methods of self-regulation and self-soothing techniques for parents to use in their parenting journey. Part two will highlight the importance of forming secure attachments with your child, and provide methods and activities to embody togetherness in the parent-child relationship. From developing rituals in the house, and building healthy boundaries using clear and concise communicative language, the parent can provide the child with a safe and secure environment. Howe highlights that 'in secure caregiver-child relationships, the caregiver is usually sensitive and thoughtful of the child's needs. They can provide care that is predictably loving, responsive, and consistent. Children with secure attachments are more likely to develop emotional intelligence, good social skills, and robust mental health.' Conscious parenting encompasses modern psychology into parenting, and as Howe demonstrates, is extremely beneficial to a child's wellbeing and mental health. More importantly, gentle parenting encourages the notion of 'holding [your child's] hand, without leading the way.'

As a final note, throughout the chapter there is an authentic understanding that every parent tries the best they can, with the resources that they have. This chapter in no way underscores the challenges which parents face whilst raising children, especially in our modern world where parenting often unintentionally takes a backseat. By choosing to become a conscious parent, you are choosing to become a better version of yourself.

Part 1: Becoming Conscious To Yourself

Heal What Hurt You

Part of becoming a conscious parent, Dr Shefali comments in her book *The Conscious Parent* is being conscious within yourself. But what does this mean?

Thich Nhat Hanh once said, 'The cry we hear from deep in our hearts comes from the wounded child within.'

Do the feelings of inadequacy in your present life stem out from a childhood where you have felt unseen and unheard? Do the feelings of abandonment come from an absent parent? Do the people pleasing attitude you suffer with come from a place of changing yourself to fit into the mould that your parents and caregivers gave to you? The roots of many of emotions we experience at present, can be traced back to our childhood, which is explored within Eastern Philosophy. Buddhists split consciousness into two parts: root consciousness, and mind consciousness.[2] The former is where our inner child lives, and the latter is where we act in our everyday life. Mindfulness is a key element when beginning self-reflection. By bringing awareness to your root consciousness and your own inner child, you become conscious within your own parenting and thus, towards your own child. This mindset helps to establish a firm boundary between who and what you may desire your child to come to,

2 Harrison, Victoria S. *Eastern philosophy: The Basics* (Routledge, 2018).

and who your child is.

Below are questions to bring awareness to your experiences, and how they may reflect within your behaviour presently.

- How would you describe your overall childhood experience?
- Was there something you loved to do as a child, which you rarely find time to do now?
- Was there any expectation from your parents regarding the way you lived your life?

Take time to explore deep into your life experiences. Are there any events which still cause you to feel an overwhelming emotion? It can be quite an isolating and lonely experience raising a child, especially as a single parent or a young parent. Having a support group, having someone to call after a tough day, someone to go out with and enjoy life away from being a parent is important to maintain a healthy and balanced mental health. The most crucial part to becoming a conscious parent is to be safe, happy and secure in the life that you have around you.

> 'The Greatest Gift that a parent can give to their child, is their own happiness.'
> – Thich Nhat Hanh, a Buddhist spiritual leader.

Break the Family Cycle of Trauma

In *It Didn't Start with You,* Mark Wolynn discusses the importance of breaking generational family trauma. He reveals that 97% of our genetic code is behavioural. That leaves less than 3% of our DNA to implement our visual characteristics such as eye colour, hair colour and skin colour. The impact of this is staggering, especially upon a closer look. Whilst your mother was a baby in her mother's belly, you were an egg in your mother's fallopian tube. This means we have a genetic behavioural code which dates back to two generations. Whilst it played a significant role in the survival of our species, in the contemporary times, we have little need of coded behaviour since we can communicate our experiences through language. Therefore, these genetic codes instead ensure unhealthy cycles are repeated within families. However, Wolynn highlights that the genetic codes received by our children is changeable. By regulation of our nervous system through deep breathing, self-soothing and overall routine of self-care, we are able to adapt our subconscious mind. By stilling our mind, we become aware of our unconscious thoughts, patterns and behaviours. This allows parents to provide a genetic 'cheat' code. Wolynn uses the example of Person A, to highlight the deep integration that our ancestors' experience in life has within our present lives.

Person A came to my therapy room, due to a recurring tendency of ending her life. She had no idea where her feelings of worthlessness and despair had come from – to her, she had lived a 'good' life, and her desire of death had her feeling hopeless, confused and filled with despair. As I began to work through her life and the history of her family, we discovered that her ancestral roots led back to Nazi Germany. Her family had been a part of the Jewish community during that time, and her grandmother was taken into the camps where she had watched her whole family die. Being the only survivor, she had felt such guilt, she had spent the rest of her days wondering why only she had been spared. Her entire being had ached for the same fate as her family, unable to process the guilt of living. Once we had uncovered this, person A's understanding of her own inner turmoil allowed her to finally process what her ancestors could not. The change in the client's emotional world was paramount. It was then I realised the importance of knowing ancestral behaviours.[3]

The severity of the above example serves to highlight how our life experiences and subconscious behaviours effect not only us, but our children and even our children's children. Through a mindful approach to your own past and the traumatic experiences you may have had, you seek to break the subconscious hold which the event has upon you and your biology. To become a conscious parent, you must become conscious of yourself.

> 'If you do not heal what is broken, then you will
> bleed on those who did not cut you.'
>
> – Mahatma Gandhi

Projecting Beliefs

Children are not an extension of their parents. Their role in life is neither to achieve the dreams that their parents could not nor Similarly, to be perfect in areas in which their parents struggle. Projection in parenting happens when

3 Wolynn, Mark. "It Didn't Start With You" Audible, 2016.

parents have not worked through their own insecurities and trauma.[4] When parents project, their inner criticism becomes their child's outer criticism. Although projection can be viewed by the parent as encouraging and guiding, if this requires the child having to live up to a dreamed perception of themselves created by their parent, then it becomes an unhealthy expectation upon the child. As a conscious parent, you remove the weight of your expectation upon your child and explore who they are together. Be curious in finding out what makes your child different to you. Do they have a better sense of direction than you? Are they more confident, or shy than you or your partner? What makes them unique? By exploring a child's identity from an early age, they can develop a better sense of self. A conscious parent allows a safe and loving space for a child to be raised, away from a preconceived idea of who and what their child should be. Dr Shefali states that our ability to accept our children is linked to our ability to accept ourself.

Self-Regulation

Children can evoke strong emotional responses within us. Having the ability to self-regulate and respond to a child's emotional chaos creates a healthier environment for both the parent and the child. As a conscious parent, you should label their trigger, 'I am feeling overwhelmed with xyz' and follow it with ten measured breaths, which allows your nervous system

---

4 Renteria, Yolanda. "Thisisyolandarenteria," Instagram, 2022, <https://www.instagram.com/p/CcRpt4tL82O/?igshid=YmMyMTA2M2Y=>

to retreat from a panicked state. Then, name the feeling: 'I am stressed/angry/frustrated.' After a few moments, reframe the problem. Rather than a parent vs child situation, switch the narrative to a parent and a child vs the problem. This creates a unified feeling to both the parent and the child, and allows a new perspective to emerge regarding the issue at hand. Using different methods of mindfulness allows the parent to access a deeper understanding of themself: a crucial element in the journey to becoming a conscious parent. Spend time with yourself, have a hobby which you enjoy doing in your spare time. Ensure you have healthy coping mechanisms in your life. Remember that you are a human being before you are a parent. Repeating affirmations to yourself, 'I am doing the best I can,' 'I am strong and caring.' You can create a sense of peace and harmony within your psyche.

Acceptance

Practicing acceptance towards yourself.

Part 2: Becoming a Conscious Parent to your Child

The Importance of Early Attachment

A child forms its most important relationships throughout its younger years. This is known as 'attachment.' Attachment is a clinical term used to describe 'a lasting psychological connectedness between human beings'.[5] This can impact both positively and negatively within an individual's life. In secure caregiver-child relationships, the caregiver is consistent with the love and security they provide to the child, and are sensitive to the child's needs. Children can form attachments with more than one caregiver, but the bond with the people who have provided close care from early infancy is the most important relationship and a long-lasting one, highlighting the importance of creating a positive and safe relationship with your child.[6] Through a conscious approach to parenting, we allow children to experience this through the important developmental stages of their life. This provides them with the tools to enter a successful relationship in the future—a healthy, happy relationship which mirrors all they experienced in their childhood. The developing attachments to their caregivers provide them with the essential tools for survival. If these attachments are not secure, this will harm the child's ability to develop. Newman states that not receiving comfort and security in the early years can have a negative

---

5 Prior, V. And Glaser, D. Understanding attachment and attachment disorders; theory, evidence and practice. London: Jessica Kinglesley, 2011

6 Bowlby, John. Attachment and loss. Volume 1: attachment. London, Pimlico, 1997, p. 87

effect on children's neurological, psychological, emotional, and physical development and functioning and vice-versa. As the opening poem connotes, parenting is about teaching a child about life, guiding them through their emotions and allowing them to embrace their full authentic self.

Being Firm, Fair and Understanding

Conscious parenting advocates for the presence of a firm and fair approach to parenting. It is often criticised for the illusion that it is permissive and boundary-less. Ryan Allen, an Early Childhood Mental Health Therapist provides a perfect example of a permissive parenting vs a gentle parenting approach. In his example (which is accessible through his TikTok profile) he highlights two different interactions:

> **One**
>
> Parent: Hey Mikey, we are about to eat. Put your phone away
>
> Child: No, I am in the game! Let me finish this first!
>
> Parent: Okay okay, finish it and then put it away. Okay?
>
> Child: Okay!
>
> * 10 minutes later*
>
> Parent: Have you still not finished your game? We want to spend time as a family.
>
> Child: Just a few more minutes!
>
> *Continues to play over time limit*

Two

Parent: Mikey, you remember the rule is no phones at the table. Put it away.

Child: No, I am in the game! Let me finish this first!

Parent: You had a 10 minute and 5-minute warning before we started eating. And you know the rule is, no phone while we are eating at the table. That way we can all spend time and talk as a family.

Child: This is not fair! This is a stupid rule. I do not want to talk to all of you!

Parent: I understand that it does not feel fair to you when you do not want to stop playing and I need you to put it away. You can put it away now and be able to play with it later or I am going to have to take it away.

Child: That is not fair! – Fine![7]

Both interactions hold loving intentions towards the child. However, number two remains firm but fair with boundaries. In the second example, the parent maintains the boundary whilst recognising and validating the child's feelings: 'I understand that it does not feel fair to you.' They then follow through with enforcing the rule: 'You can put

7 Allan, Ryan. "Pre-School Therapist," March 2022, <https://vm.tiktok.com/ZMLXn18TG/>

it away now and be able to play with it later or I am going to have to take it away.' Being a conscious parent does not mean that your child is not allowed to feel upset, hurt or wronged by you. These are important feelings for the child to understand and feel comfortable with.

They will go out into a world where these emotions and events will arise at one point or another—it is your job to teach them and guide them towards dealing with these emotions. By validating your child's experiences while enforcing a rule or boundary, you allow them to retain their autonomy. Gentle parents empathize whilst still upholding reasonable boundaries; permissive parents strive to prevent their child from feeling hurt. Giving your child boundaries will allow them to feel safe in their role. Knowing what is expected of them and having clear boundaries allows them to feel safe in the home.

Regulating Emotions

When boundaries are set, they can bring emotional responses out in the child. An essential component to becoming a conscious parent includes providing the tools to help your child regulate their emotions. When they are experiencing an intense emotion, a parent's role of maintaining calm amidst the whirlwind of the child's feelings allows the child to find a safe way of expressing and communicating about the way they feel. By giving a child the tools for handling intense emotions, the parent is enables a healthier future for the child. Having tools in your metaphorical tool belt to encourage regulation allows your child to express big feelings safely. You can do this through:

Physical Activity

- Going for a walk.
- Jumping around, or doing a silly dance.
- By taking deep breaths, and encouraging the child to do the same

Physical Touch

- Hand on the back to soothe.
- Giving your child a hug.
- Holding their hand.

You can also project an atmosphere of safety by

- Regulating your own emotions.
- Using positive body language.
- Empathetic facial expressions.[8]

Having a range of different tools within your emotional regulating tool box allows you to approach situations differently, depending on the need of the individual child; using the appropriate tool for the appropriate moment. If the only tool you own is a hammer, every situationneeds to be a nail. Help them to discover healthy ways of dealing with and expressing their emotions. This creates healthy habits for their future life.

8 Mr. Chazz, "Mr. Chazz's Leadership, Parenting and Teaching Podcast," Spotify, 2022, <http://www.patreon.com/mrchazz>

Validating Feelings

A conscious parent provides vocal validation to their child's feelings. Children love to be included. They want to know that we see and hear them—that we have time for them, that we care for them. In a society where time is very much of the essence, this is often difficult to provide for. Using and scaffolding effective communication skills is important during this time. When we cannot help them right away, letting them know makes it a little easier for them to wait. This can be communicated by setting a boundary, whilst validating and hearing their needs.

> 'I can only do one thing at a time.'
>
> 'I know it can be hard to wait. I can see how much you want me right now. I will be there soon.'
>
> 'I cannot cuddle you right now, I am doing.. Shall we find you a stuffed animal for you to cuddle while you wait?'
>
> 'I can hear you calling me! I can help in 10 minutes.'

By conscious parents providing a gentle and calm response, allowing the child to feel heard whilst also protecting their own boundaries, the child learns valuable social lessons. The same responses can be applied when dealing with siblings. Often, siblings feel jealous if they see another sibling receiving attention. By acknowledging and understanding the perspective of the child, they retain their autonomy whilst also learning the importance of perspective and patience. Communicating to your children using language which is inclusive to their perception allows them to feel heard and seen within the home, providing them with validation of their experiences in life.

Making your Home a Safe Place for Everyone

By creating an environment where the child feels seen and heard, whilst maintaining firm and gentle boundaries and allowing freedom of expression, the physicality of a house transforms into a safe place for the child to grow. Every household is different, because every family is different, since every person is different. This makes life so diverse and beautiful. Through open communication and respect for one another, a household can thrive in harmony, knowing that their sense of self is celebrated and appreciated and not forbidden and punishable. This allows the space for them to feel safe to make mistakes, enjoy the process of creating and learning and thus, develop their Growth Mindset, as coined by Carol Dweck. This mindset encourages perseverance and effort rather than natural talent and end results.

Every house will have a diverse set of values that they follow. However, blanket rules can include things such as:

- Everybody respects each other.
- Everybody has a say in the family.
- Everybody deserves to be their authentic self.

Other household rituals may include no phones during family meal times, a household rota for chores, a set day every week for a family meal or family games. These are completely interchangeable depending on household and duties. However, these must be communicated! To hold a conscious approach to parenting, it is vital that the child feels involved in the rules and rituals within the household. The most important thing you can do for your child is to create time for them within the family. A sound family unit is one of the most powerful tools that you can give your child. Time is worth more than money to your child. Giving them the opportunity to grow, make mistakes and feel comfortable in their authentic skin is paradise to a child, and a gift to their future selves. Home becomes a place where everybody feels valued, heard, and respected. Having rules and rituals which create an environment of togetherness brings harmony within the family—a true cornerstone to the conscious approach to parenting.

Rituals

Rituals, in a similar way to rules, create a routine and an expectation in the house. Whereas rules are strictly enforced, rituals are encouraged. They bring the family together in moments of laughter, fun and acceptance. Encourage your child to write their thoughts down in a daily or weekly journal. Children love to copy, so if you maintain a journal, chances are that your child will be more than eager to join you in writing down the events of the day. The entire family could meet on a Sunday afternoon for half an hour, to write and reflect upon their week. This would be a fantastic opportunity to create and set intentions for the week ahead. It is also a creative way for a family to celebrate and reflect on experiences and emotions with each other, after a busy week. Rituals of togetherness are an important way of maintaining a child's sense of connection.[9] Whether you gather for breakfast in the morning before school, or reserve a family cuddle every Sunday morning. Reiterate the importance of togetherness. By creating and maintaining the rituals in the family, the child develops important social and emotional skills, along with a secure sense of being. Creating a family environment which celebrates everyone for their uniqueness is a binding force in the child's psyche. Their sense of self is firmly rooted within their psyche, due to their secure relationships formed within their early years. A conscious parent creates loving and creative rituals within the house, reserving time for their family and creating quality moments.

Spending Quality Time

It is the quality of a connection to your child, which provides them with the confidence to live a meaningful and authentic life. A conscious parent ensures that quality time is the foundation of forming a positive relationship with their child. By embodying this, a parent shows the child that they are worthy of their time and affection.

Provide a meaningful narrative for your child.

Children count on us to help them make sense of their reality. Our task is to teach them—through our actions and our language—how to find meaning and purpose in life. A subtle, yet powerful way we can do this is by spending time with them. Your presence is their continuality. Your emotional connection and presence help them to feel loved

---

9 Shefali, 347.

and secure.[10] Storytelling provides a wonderful opportunity for this. Not only are you spending quality time with your child, you are also giving them an interpretative framework to help them understand and process events which may have occurred in their life. You are not only reading to them, but also demonstrating them the power of a unique, personal story. Make stories the medium to show how brave they are, how kind they are. Share appropriate stories of your life with them. If they are struggling with a situation at school, make it into a story. Ask them, what would the main character do? Allow them to explore their reality through a different lens. When children hear about themselves in a story, they can understand and relate through an alternate perspective, better absorbing what you are attempting to convey. By helping them weave a narrative about themselves, and their place in the family and society you give them a sense of purpose within life. Conscious parenting encourages the child to find their own authenticity and path within life, taking them by the hand but allowing them to lead the way.

Creating a Conscious Space

A conscious parent creates spaces for the child to find stillness. Allowing your child to feel comfortable and peaceful in these moments, create an aura of tranquillity within both you and your child. Dr Shefali encourages parents to create an environment for the child where they can sit in silence. Moments spent in the car are great opportunities to create

---

10 Shefali, 318.

this space. By driving in each other's silence, your child's nervous system takes a break from the constant distraction provided from the outside world. They become familiar with moments of calm. And thus, they are more likely to bring their comfort with quiet into their everyday lives. This develops their ability to observe, which allows them great insight into themselves. Of course, this does not mean that every moment should be spent in solitude or that we stop engaging with our children. Rather, a parent should be aware that there is a balance between engagement and dis-engagement, doing and not doing. Shefali observes, 'moments of solitude and stillness are not empty moments, though they may feel like it initially. They are moments of fullness, where we experience the presence of our being for contemplation and reflection.'[11] By guiding a child to observe their thoughts and feelings, they become confident in labelling and expressing emotions. A conscious parent creates an environment where their child feels safe to do so.

Teenage Years

Teenage years are difficult. They are accompanied by a rebellious nature and an indifference to family life, focusing on friendship and developing relationships outside of the home.[12] Children belong less to their parents now than they ever did. Therefore, the dynamic of the relationship between them changes. Parents need to understand that their child is

11 Shefali, 458.

12 Cox, Brain. "The Infinite Monkey Cage," BBC Radion 4, Spotify. 2021.

growing and therefore they need to be given autonomy. The teenage years are dedicated to growth and transformation for a child, and your relationship with them may begin to move away from the parent centered one they required when they were younger. This is due to several chemical reactions which are happening within your teenagers' brain. One of these is called differentiation. Differentiation is a process that occurs organically between the ages of 13–21, but does have fluidity and may operate outside of the give age frame.[13] During this stage, after being guided and moulded by the opinions and beliefs of their parents, teenagers have a natural urge to explore their own individuality. The foundation of differentiation is 'I want to know who I am.' During this stage, it is natural for teens to explore various parts of themselves. This is when we see teens dye their hair, ask for piercings, paint their rooms a colour their parents do not understand, wear clothing their parents do not like, and explore and experiment with various parts of their identity. In healthy differentiation, a parent carefully acknowledges and accepts differentiation, while also building healthy limits and boundaries. The result of healthy differentiation is an adult who has their own identity, values, and beliefs. If a teen is unable to express their changing identity, they grow up without a sense of identity, and frequently look to others for validation. This is because they have learned to not trust their own intuition on what they like and what they do not. This leads them to

13 Renteria, Yolanda. Instagram, 2022. <https://www.instagram.com/p/CcRpt4tL82O/?igshid=YmMyMTA2M2Y=>

incline more towards dominant relationships, whether that be a friendship or a loving relationship. These relationships tend to have a huge power differential at best, and can be abusive and manipulative at worst. Lack of differentiation is more likely to happen with strict parents who are not willing to let their children explore anything which leaves the parent feeling uncomfortable. These parents tend to have rigid rules and expectations on who their children should be, how they should act and the people that they associate with. The teenagers become afraid of punishment, and a loss of connection to their parents. They need you to hold their hand, but no longer need you to lead the way. By remaining present throughout their struggles, guiding them safely through their desire to explore new experiences and identities, you can grow and develop your relationship in a whole, new, and exciting way.

Giving Gratitude

Finally, showing gratitude to children, especially as a parent generates feelings of appreciation and worthiness. Dr Shefali states that when teaching parents about gratitude, you are handing them one of the most powerful techniques to use within parenting. Expressing gratitude reminds a child of their worth—that they are a valuable person in your life. Gratitude to your child also reminds them that life is kind, caring and filled with love and appreciation. This is an essential mindset to live a happy and healthy life. CBT (Cognitive Behavioural Therapy) therapy highlights the link between an individual's mindset and the quality of their life. If a child has a confident, healthy perception of themselves, their quality of life will reflect this. Joe Despenza argues that your personality, reflects your personal-reality.[14]

Create a game around the table, see who can name more things that they are grateful for. Our ability to notice and appreciate the smallest elements in life encourages them to slow down and enjoy the moments in life, no matter how small. Such gratitude enables them to foster a positive mindset in the world around them. Additionally, by celebrating the child and being vocal in your gratitude to them just for being them, you are building them up to be secure, happy adults. Children are rarely acknowledged and thanked for being themselves, yet parents expect their children to acknowledge them for everything that they do. By giving your child a meaningful 'thank you,' you can encourage their self-confidence and worth, to grow and expand. In this way you communicate their intrinsic value, just for being themselves.

How different our world would be if we had all been brought up with this value!

Summary

Conscious parenting requires a continuous journey of self-discovery and moment to moment presence for the parent and the child. Both are on the journey together. The conscious approach is a living, breathing and loving method which exists within every moment in every day. Every day presents a new challenge—a new lesson to be learnt. By allowing yourself to grow alongside your child, opening yourself up to

---

14 Despenza, Joe. "Breaking the Habit of Being Yourself." Audible, 2021.

the experiences they offer to life, you are not only embracing the unknown parts of yourself but also providing a template for your child to copy. By embodying the characteristics and traits that you wish your child to have, you are providing them with a safe and secure role model whom they may look up to. It is the parent who establishes the child's view of the world, and therefore, also is the parent who needs to breach their unconscious behaviour. It is the parent that shapes the habits of the child, who teaches them how to be self-critical by voicing their insecurity around the child, who teaches them to doubt themself when being critical of their opinions and thoughts—how to love and not love, based on whether we love ourselves. To detach from an unconscious habit is not easy, but it is what is required to become a more conscious, effective parent. How fulfilling a child's life will be, is dependent on their connection with their parent. Rather than looking for outward experiences to fill their souls, they will already have what they need within them. They will be at peace with who they are. The way we can meet ourself, and meet our own needs in our life is reflective of the level at which you are able to consciously meet your child.

Remind your child how important they are to you. Remind them of their importance in your life. Remind them that even though life may be difficult and they may walk through tough times, they are still worthy of love and care. Be the person in the child's life who can see and hear them, who comforts them when they cry, who reads to them before bed. Teach them what it feels like to be accepted for who they are—to embrace their uniqueness and make it their superpower. More importantly, find a moment every day to build upon your connection to your child. Ask them questions about their life, and listen authentically and attentively to their response.

Children see life through a rose-coloured lens and they love unconditionally. They are a joy to have in life, and they bring magic to even the most mundane of days. Their imagination, perseverance and intelligence are second to none. Marvel at the world with them. And love them unconditionally and authentically.

AZURA ABRASID
Early Childhood Education Programme Leader in Veritas University College, Kuala Lumpur, Malaysia.

As an Early Childhood Education Programme Leader at the Veritas University College, Azura Abrasid designs and conducts professional training for future early childhood educators. Her unwavering passion for Early Childhood Education has influenced generations of preschool teachers since 2008. She loves conducting and learning from educational research but finds that her best lessons are when she is surrounded by children.

TEN

PARENTS AS PARTNERS IN EARLY CHILDHOOD EDUCATION

ALMOST TWO decades ago, I left the kindergarten where I was working as coordinator because I felt frustrated in making very little difference in children's lives. I changed my career to working with adults, initially as a Lecturer of Early Childhood Education and later as a professional program designer for practitioners, thinking that my scope to enhance children's lives would be greater by working with stakeholders in the industry.

Working for several years in tertiary education and doing quite a handful of community work related to hands-on parent involvement and community development, I realize that it is not a question of working with either children or adults but a question of working with both together—parents and children are both the key to improving the well-being and learning of children.

This chapter is about the intensive work between Early Childhood Education practitioners and parents. It explores why it is important, how the relationship can be improved, and what are the challenges in this partnership. The chapter is of interest to any practitioner who works with parents and wants to extend their practice in this area, as well as parents making this chapter valuable resources in understanding the parental partnership in improving their child's learning and development.

Although the central focus for chapter is on the adults in a child's life, it strives to be as significant to children as well. The whole purpose of the partnership between a professional and a parent is the well-being, learning and development of the child.

The central focus of this chapter is the parent, in order for the practitioners to explore how they can work with parents to engage them deeply in their childr's learning while also addressing their own aspirations, growth and development.

Depending on practitioners' experience and the context they work in, much of the contents of this chapter may already be familiar to some and the work with parents may seem quite ordinary. Or many of the ideas and suggestions may be completely new and some would feel overwhelmed by how difficult the work with parents appears to be. Working with parents is a regular interaction with a fellow human. It can be as complex, at times demanding, challenging, and sometimes very frustrating, but it is highly stimulating, moving and often greatly rewarding. Most importantly, it makes a real difference to the children we all work with.

'Family engagement is about the way you think.'
(Epstein, Joyce 2009)

The Term 'Parents'

The importance of a parent's role in a child's life is crucial and clearly acknowledged. There is a growing understanding and several evidence from studies conducted, that parents' views should be heard more and taken into consideration especially in the Early Childhood Education sector and throughout children's schooling (Desforges and Abouchaar, 2003, Siraj-Blatchford et al, 2002). To achieve it, parents should have the opportunity to engage actively with their child and get involved in meaningful and relevant ways in their children's early experiences in Early Childhood Education centres, pre-schools, toddler groups and schools. In the meantime, practitioners in the children's workforce are aware that they need to understand the child's home and family environment much better to be able to effectively nurture and support their teaching and learning, well-being, and development. Much of the knowledge about the child which practitioners require is held by the parents. Hence practitioners, must develop strong and trusting relationships with them to be able to access those.

Before exploring the relationship between practitioners and parents, one must delve into the meaning of the term 'parent'. From the Guidance to the Standards for the Award of Early Years Professional Status (Children's Workforce Development Council [CWDC], 2008) parents are described as, 'Mothers, fathers, legal guardians, and the primary caretakers of looked-after children.' (CWDC, 2008, p78). The Guidance continues to point out that there may also be other significant adults in a child's life, for example a grandparent, an aunt or the new partner of the child's mother. These adults may spend a lot of time with a child, develop loving and supportive relationships with him/her and are generally seen as being responsible for him/her. They may also be the point of contact for the practitioner with the child's family and may be able to assist the practitioner to learn about the environment in the child's home.

For the purposes of this chapter and the practical work of engaging with parents, it will be useful to employ a wider definition of the term 'parents' than the one arising from the understanding of parental responsibility. In addition to mothers, fathers, legal guardians, and the primary caretakers, we will therefore, also include other significant adults in a child's life in this term.

Practitioners' Views of Parents

Studies by Rodd (2006) stated that Early Childhood Education practitioners and parents alike develop their beliefs about children in their families of origin. Developing beliefs and values in life often means that we see them as facts without considering whether they are true or not. In USA, Anti-Bias Curriculum are widely used as it provides the practitioners tools to work with children to address pre-prejudice and stereotypes. It stresses how early the foundations are laid for later prejudices and the harm they can do to a child's development by narrowing his/her view of other people and his/her reluctance to engage with them (Derman-Sparks and the ABC Task Force, 1993). It is important for

Early Childhood Education practitioners to recognize pre-prejudice and early stereotypes in the play and behaviour of young children and address them. However, partitioners may not have the same level of awareness for stereotypes and beliefs which were formed in their own childhood and are the basis of their current actions and behaviour.

The relationship between Early Childhood Education practitioners and parents are special, as parents entrust the care for their dearest and most vulnerable relative—their child—to practitioners. They expect the practitioners to focus their energies on facilitating their child's development, growth and well-being. However, it cannot be done without assistance from the parents, since, most of the population, Early Childhood Education practitioners have personal views of parents, which may impact on the way they perceive and interact with them.

Given any situation, it would be very hard to build trusting and supportive relationships if one partner held negative or misplaced views of the other. In common interest of children, it is extremely important that practitioners approach parents with positive attitudes as there is a correlation between practitioners' views of parents and parents' views of practitioners. Knopf and Swick (2007) found that when practitioners see parents more positively, parents feel better about their care and teaching. Consequently, the levels of parents' involvement in their child's learning in the Early Childhood Education setting increases. Exploring and addressing the stereotypes found amongst practitioners is therefore, essential to create the right environment and ethos in which positive relationships can flourish. Knopf and Swick

(2007) found that some practitioners thought that parents did not care, that they did not have the time or motivation to get involved and/or that they were not interested in leadership roles. Some practitioners may argue that their own experience shows these assumptions to be true, in most cases, an exploration of how they have tried to engage with parents and encourage them to get involved may be useful.

Once practitioners are aware of their own assumptions and prejudices. They can evaluate how they influence their practice and relationships with parents. Practitioners may now also be in a better position to recognize the assumptions colleagues make about parents and stimulate the discussion about how the issues could be overcome. For a team of practitioners to work effectively together it is fundamental to share the same basic values and beliefs and not to let personal views and individual prejudices result in mixed messages to parents and children. Rather than tackling individual counterproductive assumptions practitioners may want to take a more positive approach and explore their setting's overall ethos with regards to parents and collaborate with other practitioners to learn their underlying principles and how these are expressed in their practice.

Rodd (2006) in her study, further summarizes that values and beliefs are fundamental for the development of practitioner's partnership with parents. She addresses these lists of assumptions of parents as a good starting point:

- Parents are experts on their children
- Parents are significant and effective teachers of their own children

- Parents are skilled in ways that complement those of practitioners
- Parents are different but have equal strengths and equivalent expertise
- Parents are inherently involved in the lives and well-being of their children
- Parents can contribute to and central in decision-making
- Parents can make informed observations and impart vital information to practitioners
- Parents are responsible and share accountability with practitioners

Triangular Relationship between Parents, Children and Practitioners

Naturally, children develop their first relationships with their parents. These are crucial as parents are the secure base for children's emotional and social development that provide models for their fore coming relationships. When children come into Early Childhood Education settings, they develop new relationships with their designated practitioners. But these relationships are shaped by their former experiences. Both parents and practitioners are two very significant beings in a child's life which affect not just his/her childhood development but also his/her well-being in later years. Therefore, it is important that parent and practitioners work closely together and set the same expectations and boundaries at home and in Early Childhood Education setting.

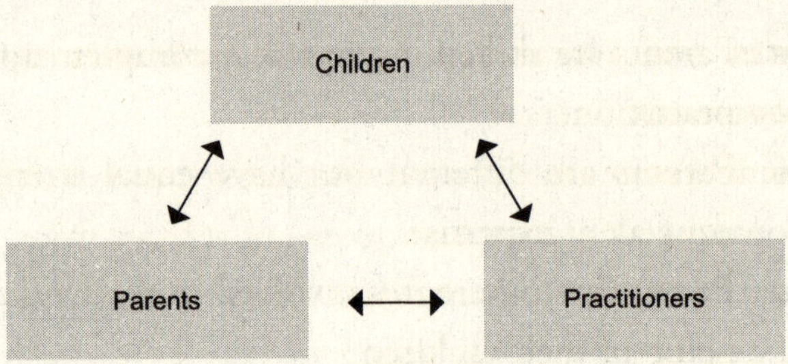

Figure 1. Early Childhood Education: Triangular Relationship between Parents, Children and Practitioners

The above figure portrays the dynamic relationship between the parents, children, and practitioners. In the child-parent relationship, early attachment is particularly important as it influences children's continuing well-being and positive achievements. Meanwhile the relationship between child and practitioner correlates to their adjustment at school. Because of this crucial importance of a child's relationship with his/her parent, Early Childhood Education settings should support the development of good parenting skills and facilitate access to family support services.

As for the relationship between practitioners and parents, the life experiences and backgrounds of parents are characterized by great variety. Due to this factor, practitioners need to be very flexible in their approach to parents and use a range of different methods and strategies. Practitioners should explore parents' expectations of them, and identify parents' wish to engage and work together. In enabling parental expectations, it may be necessary to provide training opportunities for new practitioners as their lack of experience in the work with adults often acts as a barrier to the successful engagement with parents.

Parents and Home Environment Influence on Child's Achievement

Bronfenbrenner's theory on ecological systems describes child development as a complex system of relationships which is affected by his/her surroundings. Our own experience is likely to tell us that most of our beliefs and values resemble those of the family we grew up in. This stresses the importance of the experiences in early childhood and the influence parents have on children's lives. Research confirms that the environment at home and parental involvement in learning activities have a substantial influence on a child's attainment in learning and development. Siraj-Blatchford et al. (2002) summaries that the involvement of parents in learning activities is linked to better cognitive attainment in child's initial years. In supporting cognitive development, the quality of learning environment at home also greatly influences the social development of children (Daycare Trust, 2003). Desforges and Abouchaar (2003) whose research focused on children achievement and attainment, have found that parental involvement in their child's learning at home has a significant effect on the child's achievements. In fact, the effect is greater than the quality of the schools teaching and learning. Their research also highlights that parents' involvement is more in their child's life when the child achieves more.

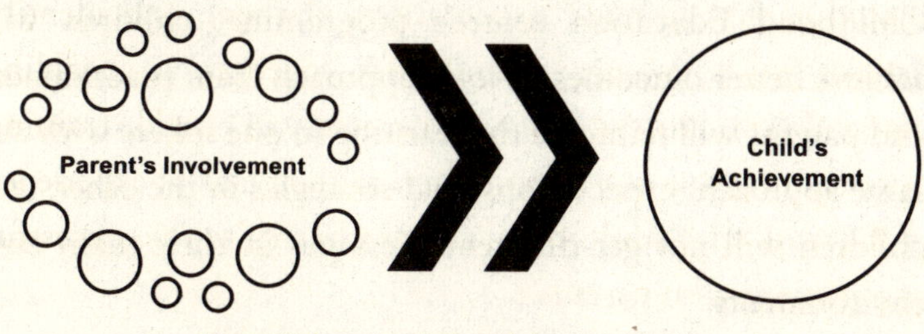

Figure 2. Parent and Child Motivational Cycle

Parents seem to be motivated by the success of their children and feel encouraged to continue their involvement in their child's learning and development. Additionally, parental participation also leads to a positive effect on how teachers perceive a child—it increases the teacher's expectations of the child (Einarsdottir and Gardarsdottir, 2009). This in turn encourages the child to perform better and hence, increases her academic achievements.

Figure 3. Parent, Teacher and Child Motivational Cycle

This highlights how interrelated parent, child and Early Childhood Education practitioners are and how they influence one another's behavior. It brings us to the conclusion that Early Childhood Education practitioners must work closely with parents as this enhances their work with children and improves the outcomes for children. Siraj-Blatchford et al. (2002) added that where there is consensus and consistency between the learning at home and the Early Childhood Education centre's programme, children will achieve better outcomes. A joint approach from practitioners and parents will reinforce the learning in one sphere with the same approach, expectations, and strategies in the other, and children will not get different messages in their main care environments.

How do Studies Define Parental Involvement?

Joyce Epstein and her colleagues at the Center on Family, School, and Community Partnerships at Johns Hopkins University, developed a useful framework, defining six ways in which parent are involved. Figure 4. next page shows the involvement of parents in Early Childhood Education.

Most researchers condensed these lists into parent involvement at home and at Early Childhood Education centre, using definitions such as:

- Engaging in play and learning activities at home, including helping with reading skills.
- Supervising and monitoring child's milestone at home
- Talking about day-to-day activities as the centre.
- Attending centre events, going to parent-teacher conferences, meeting with teachers, and volunteering in centre activities.

As Epstein describes, parental involvement is vital to the success of children, their learning and development. Efforts involving parents as partners are becoming more and more prevalent in today's Early Childhood education centre as practitioners look for innovative ways to engage even the most hard-to-reach parents.

Lewin and Luckin (2010) found that participatory technologies can be especially engaging for parents, but practitioners have to use the technology purposefully and sensitively to meet the complex needs of stakeholders across contexts.

Type of Involvement	General Description	Involvement in Early Childhood Education
Parenting	Assist families with parenting and child-rearing skills, understanding child and adolescent development, and setting home conditions that support children as students at each age and grade level. Assist schools in understanding families.	• Discussing child's development • Doing things together (play, meals) • Supporting development
Communicating	Communicate with families about school programs and student progress through effective school-to-home and home-to-school communications.	• Parents initiated contacts about child's development • Centre initiated contacts about child's learning and development
Supporting	Improve recruitment, training, work, and schedules to involve families as volunteers and audiences at the school or in other locations to support students and school programs.	• Volunteering • Attending center activities
Learning at home	Involve families with their children in learning activities at home, including homework and other curriculum-linked activities and decisions.	• Encouraging continuation of learning and development at home (literacy skills etc.)
Decision making	Include families as participants in school decisions, governance, and advocacy, school councils, committees, and other parent organizations.	• Taking part in parents' partnership or organization
Collaborating with community	Coordinate resources and services for families, students, and the school with businesses, agencies, and other groups, and provide services to the community.	• Communicating parents to parents

Figure 4. Parental Involvement in Early Childhood Education: Epstein's Framework

What Parents Gain from Getting Involved?

Most parents want to do the best for their children and are prepared to sacrifice their own interests, leisure time or convenience for this purpose. Getting involved and being more active in their child's life and in the community, they live in has positive effects for the parents as well.

A study by the National Institute of Adult Continuing Learning and the Pre-school Learning Alliance highlighted the benefits of parental involvement. According to the study, many parents reported making new social contacts, which enabled them to overcome feelings of isolation due to parenting stress and helping them to develop support networks. This can limit poor mental health and depression. Furthermore, finding shows that parents became more confident and took initiatives to undertake learning opportunities and consider employment. Communication, social and practical skills are all increased. Another significant finding was that parents who left school early and had few qualifications, first time parents, and parents with limited experience of employment made the greatest gains through involvement at pre-school (McGivney, 1998). These research findings clearly show that parents benefit greatly from their involvement in Early Childhood Education, as far as their own development is concerned.

Children simultaneously gained from their parents' involvement in their Early Childhood Education setting as parents felt more confident in their parenting role. Talking to other parents and seeing a group of children helped them to put their own and their child's experiences into perspective. In addition, most involved parents reported that they had learned to organize, structure, and manage children's play and had acquired an understanding of how children learn through play. As a result, parents were able to stimulate their own children in more creative ways at home and as well as improved their parents-child relationships.

Why is it Important for Practitioners to Work with Parents?

One of Early Childhood Education goal is to prepare children for school readiness. School readiness is foundational across Early Childhood systems and programs. It means children are ready for school, families are ready to support their children's learning, and schools are ready for children. Most of Early Childhood systems and programs views school readiness as children possessing the skills, knowledge, and attitudes necessary for success in school and for later learning and life. Physical, cognitive, social, and emotional development are all essential ingredients of school readiness. It is then said, practitioners and parents play an important role in creating enriching and supportive learning environments for young children to achieve this goal.

Sometimes practitioners see the need to work well with parents just as one more demand in their work scope. They might think, aren't children the focus of their work? Why should they dilute their energy and effort to focus on the parents as well? So, why is it important for them to work with parents? Because it's the best thing for children. Children gain the most from their early education experience when a partnership exists between practitioners and parents.

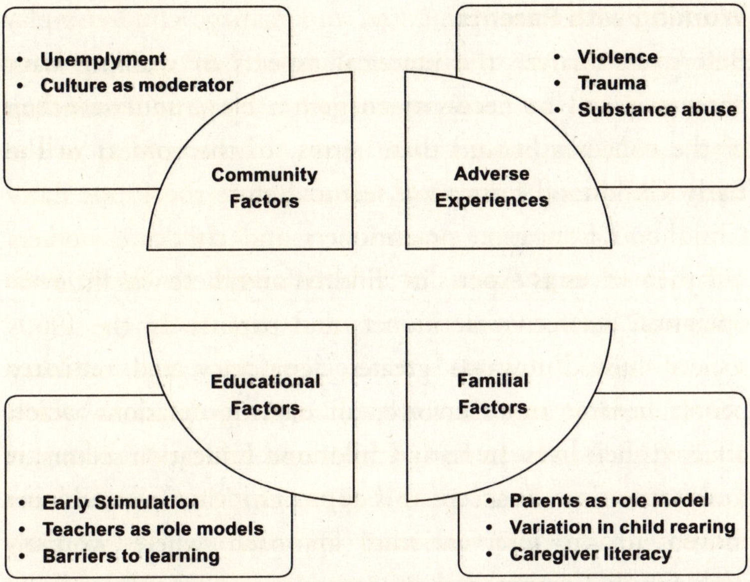

Figure 5: Themes that Impact Children's School Readiness

As an Early Childhood Education professional, practitioners have a lot to offer parents. They usually have special insight into the needs and interest of children. Practitioners can help parents differentiate between issues that are related to general development and issues that are specific to their children. They also can help parents to keep their expectations to age appropriate and offer parents solutions to any struggles they may be having with their children.

Parents vice versa have a lot to offer practitioners as well. Parents know their children well; they may help practitioners find the strategies to best teach their children. They know their children's preferences and abilities and able to read their children's feelings. Practitioners' jobs will be easier in partnership with parents.

Working with Parents

Before we analyze the practical aspects of working with parents it will be necessary to gain a clear understanding of the concepts behind these terms, in the context of the Early Childhood Education sector. Before the 1960s Early Childhood Education practitioners and childcare workers saw themselves as experts in children and there was little co-operation between practitioners and parents. In the 1960s society moved towards greater democracy and ordinary people became more involved in making decisions which affected their lives. In Early Childhood Education sectors, it took some time to accept this approach. Most practitioners moved to an interventionist approach where working with families assumed that something was missing in the families which practitioners had to supply. This, however, did not recognize the contributions parents make to their children's lives and did not allow meaningful co-operation to develop between practitioners and parents. In the 1970s, communication was brought to the forefront. Early Childhood Education's practitioners recognized that parents would be more comfortable interacting with them, if they communicated often and hence, eventually develop positive relationship with them.

This drastically changed the philosophy of accountability in the 1980s. Parents were seen as consumers of a service and Early Childhood Education settings began to work towards meeting their demands and wishes. At this stage, parental involvement focused on consultation and discussion of policies and procedures. The belief that parents had the right to control decisions that affected their children became embedded, leading to a demand for effective participation and active management by parents in the 1990s. The 1980s and 1990s also brought the recognition that parents were experts as far as their own children were concerned, leading most Government expecting true work of partnership with parents in Early Childhood Education (Rodd, 2006, Arnold, 2008).

> 'Parental involvement takes many forms including good parenting in the home, the provision of a secure and stable environment, intellectual stimulation, parent–child discussion, good models of constructive social and educational values and high aspirations relating to personal fulfilment and good citizenship; contact with schools to share information; participation in school events; participation in the work of the school; and participation in school governance.'
>
> (Desforges and Abouchaar, 2003, p4)

In the light interpretations of the term 'involvement' and 'partnership' it seems necessary to clarify in the ways parents become a part of this dynamic. It could be their children's learning in the widest sense, or classroom activities like reading with children, or managerial tasks as committee member. It is also worth noting that practitioners and parents may associate different contexts with the term. Practitioners tend to think of involvement as a centre-based activity which relates to children's learning or support in the classroom. Parents on the other hand, usually view 'involvement' in much broader terms, often relating the notion that includes wide activities and engagement with community outside the school (Knopf and Swick, 2007).

Involving parents in Early Childhood Education setting and in their children's teaching and learning experiences is the first step which will, through the development of trusting relationships and over a certain time, lead to a partnership between parent and practitioners.

According to Rodd (2006) principles of effective partnership in an Early Childhood Education setting are as follows:

- It is a non-hierarchical, collaborative relationship.
- Both practitioners and parents are experts as far as children are concerned.
- Practitioners and parents share responsibility for the children.

The partnership concept between parents and practitioners should be equals, in which both make valuable contributions and neither dominates the other. Both parents and practitioners should have an equal interest in the child's well-being, learning, development, and decisions are made based on negotiation.

Building Parent-Practitioner Relationships

The process of building relationships with parents requires some time, however, once good relationships are formed, practitioners find it easier to talk to parents about more sensitive issues regarding their children—for example, their child's aggressive behavior. It is important for practitioners to be inclusive and non-discriminatory in their efforts to build relationships. When there are language barriers, practitioners must find ways to overcome it, for the family to not feel not excluded. Some parents may prefer spoken information, while others respond better to written information. Hence, practitioners may have to employ different means of communication to ensure effective communication.

Once parents access Early Childhood Education setting, practitioners must continue developing the relationship with them to get them involved in more activities or in detailed discussions about their children's learning, which forms better partnership with them.

Much of this relationship is defined by practitioners' values regarding parents and families and practitioners' attitude towards them. A huge factor in building successful relationship with parents is the way practitioners communicate with parents. The following image addressed some principles for successful daily interactions with parents.